Swallow Irritation Before Irritation Swallows You

Swallow Irritation Before Irritation Swallows You

JP VASWANI

wisdom tree

ISBN 978-81-8328-450-9

Published by
Wisdom Tree
4779/23, Ansari Road
Darya Ganj, New Delhi-110 002
Ph.: 23247966/67/68
wisdomtreebooks@gmail.com

Printed in India

Contents

Part III: Staying Rooted In Calmness

PART I

How Irritation Swallows Us

1

Why are We Unhappy?

We live in stirring times. The twenty-first century represents, indeed, the age of technology. Many of us do not climb staircases anymore—we take the elevator. Wherever we are—on a bus, train, or out on a walk—we keep in touch with our friends, family, clients and customers on the mobile phone.

We exchange masses of information across the globe by means of email and the internet. We have bigger, better, faster cars to drive; better and more expensive clothes to wear; time and labour-saving gadgets in our kitchen. Economists tell us that lifestyles are improving; the quality of life, they say, is getting better, whatever that means. Per capita income, we are told, is rising. GDP is improving…

We have everything except happiness and peace of mind! We have practically everything we want—more money, more food, more clothes, more comforts; we have powerful aircrafts, luxury automobiles, we have air conditioners, DVD players, hi-fi systems, HDTVs, MP3 players—the list is endless. We are surrounded by comforts and conveniences that our ancestors could never ever have visualised.

And yet we are not happy!

There was once a *brahmachari,* a humble mendicant, who lived in a temple on the outskirts of a town. He lived an austere and dedicated life. He spent his time studying the scriptures, reciting Vedic mantras, meditating under a huge banyan tree or doing yogic asanas. He got his food from begging for he was committed to living on the alms of the charitable ones.

One day, the king of the realm visited the temple. Soldiers lined the road, decorated elephants led the royal procession and the royal chariot was drawn by six magnificent horses.

When the *brahmachari* saw the grandeur and pomp, the sheer splendour of the king's retinue, he said to himself, 'Surely, this must be the happiest man in the world!'

As the king was leaving the temple after worship, the *brahmachari* bowed down to him and said with deep respect, 'Sir, may I ask you something?'

The king was in a happy and congenial mood. 'Ask what you will,' he said to the young man. 'I will do my best to give you an appropriate answer.'

'O King,' said the *brahmachari,* 'tell me, is it not true that you are one of the happiest men in the world?'

'Ah!' sighed the king. 'How I wish it were true! But you are mistaken. It is true that I have everything that world can give—I am a master of pleasures, possessions, power and pelf. But I cannot call myself a happy man! I do not have a son who can succeed to my throne after me! I am childless, and the best physicians in the realm tell me that I will never

ever be able to father my own children. Is this not enough to make any man unhappy?

'However, if you want to meet the happiest man in my kingdom, I will tell you whom you should meet. There is a wealthy merchant who lives in the capital. His name is Vijayadutta. He is blessed with three tall, strapping, splendid boys. He lives in a palatial house and is attended by a hundred servants. It is obvious that he is a happy man indeed!'

Days passed, and one morning, the *brahmachari* was informed that the wealthy merchant, Vijayadutta, was to visit the temple that day. He was delighted to hear it, for he had been longing to meet him. When the merchant came out of the temple after darshan, the *brahmachari* met him and said, 'Sir, I have been told that you are one of the happiest men in the kingdom; not only are you wealthy and powerful, but you have also been blessed with three sons! You live in a palatial house, you have servants at your beck and call. You have everything a man can desire. Is it not true that you are the happiest of men?'

'*Arre Brahmachari*,' sighed the merchant, taking the young man aside. 'If only you knew the truth! Yes, yes, I do have three sons—but they are rascals of the worst order! They are plundering all my wealth; they are robbing me of all peace and comfort. I shudder even to say this to you…' and he wiped the tears from his eyes before he went on. 'I shudder to say this, but they are just waiting for me to die, so that they can take control of my hard-earned wealth and squander it all away!'

Overwhelmed by grief, the merchant could not speak. After a while, he continued, 'You will not believe me when I say this: I wish I had no son at all!'

The *brahmachari* gazed at the grieving merchant in blank amazement. How deceptive appearances could be!

'Let me tell you about the happiest man in the city,' the merchant told him. 'There is a pundit who teaches the children of a school. He dwells in a humble cottage just outside the school. But he is adored by all his students. They follow him wherever he goes, and they catch every word that drops from his lips for they treasure his words like pearls of wisdom. Surely, that learned, intelligent and respected pundit must be the happiest man on earth!'

Now, the *brahmachari* had often seen the pundit visiting the temple in the past. But he was not to be seen now. However, one of his students was a regular visitor to the temple. So the next time he visited, the *brahmachari* approached him and asked, 'Is it true that your learned teacher is the happiest man on earth? I long to ask him this question, but I don't see him here these days. Will you ask him if this is indeed the truth?'

The student met the teacher the next day and asked him, 'Sir, is it true that you are one of the happiest men on earth?'

'Ah!' sighed the pundit. 'I have burnt the midnight oil; I have weakened my eyes and wasted the best years of my life acquiring knowledge. I struggle to pass it on to my students, but if only you knew the meagre salary I receive for this task, you will pity me! It is not possible for me to make two ends meet. How could you ever imagine that I would be the happiest man on earth?

'However, if you wish to see the happiest man in these parts, I can direct you to him. Do you know the temple on the outskirts of the town? Go there, and you will find a young mendicant, a *brahmachari* who lives an utterly dedicated life of simple living and high thinking. If only you could see the radiant smile playing upon his lips, the light of peace and tranquillity that emanates from his eyes! I have always found him happy, serene and carefree. He has no anxieties, no worries whatsoever! He has no family to support. He does not even care to know where his next meal is coming from! I do believe that he must be the happiest of men.'

I really do not know whether this got back to the *brahmachari* and if it did, I cannot imagine what his reaction would have been! But I do know this, we are all apt to imagine that others are always happy and always happier than us!

Yes, every one of us wants to be happy, but we don't know why we are not happy. We are all engaged in the same quest—it is our one great desire to be happy. Why then, are we not?

I believe we are not happy because we do not have peace of mind, we do not have peace in the heart within.

A holy man, who lived centuries ago, made this statement: 'Nothing in the morn have I and nothing do I have at night. Yet, there is none on earth happier than I!'

When they asked him how this was possible, he said, 'It is because I have a peaceful mind.'

How many of us can make such a claim? How many of us enjoy that great gift—peace of mind?

The Gita says: *Ashantasya kutah sukham!* How can a man be happy if there is no peace in his heart!

We have all that we need and more; some of us have everything we could ever think of, sometimes, two of everything! A friend recently told me that an announcement had been made in his residential society that no resident would be allowed to park more than two cars in the society's parking lot.

'And are there many residents with two cars?' I asked him.

'I'm afraid some families have three cars, Dada,' he told me.

'And what would they do with three cars?' I wondered aloud, for I am a simple person and I live a simple life.

'But Dada, the father needs his car to attend to his business. The children need to be dropped and picked up from school. They need to go to their dancing, swimming lessons, their tennis practice and also visit their own friends. And the wives and mothers have their shopping and their kitty parties to go to. After all, one has to think of everything!'

I quietly listened to what he said. After a little pause, my friend continued.

'Naturally Dada, many of my neighbours are upset and annoyed about the society's decision. We have spent millions of rupees to acquire a comfortable home with a prestigious address. Of what use is it if we are forced to put up with such irritating restrictions?'

Never before have we had such material wealth and property and yet, we are unhappy!

I belong to the Sindhi community, many of whom were forced to leave behind everything they possessed when Partition divided our country into two. Many brothers and sisters crossed the new border to come into India with little more than the clothes on their back. Leave alone one or two cars for the family, many of them did not so much as have a roof over their head!

We now have all that the human heart can desire—entertainment at the touch of a button, exotic meals a phone call away, instant communication and more leisure time than we can handle constructively. We are the legatees of the great age of technology, but we are not happy! We are permanently dissatisfied, and we suffer from a million ailments like heart attacks, high blood pressure, nervous breakdowns, ulcers, stress and whatnot.

We have everything, except a peaceful mind. And truly has it been said, happiness is in the mind, not in objects. Money can give us lots of things; in fact, people say money can buy anything but money cannot buy you happiness. For happiness is not an object; it is a state of mind. It cannot be purchased; it can only be experienced.

Yes, happiness is what all of us yearn for, but few of us realise.

I have always believed that happiness is our birthright, and if we want, we can always achieve it!

In a book called *Inspired Talks,* Swami Vivekananda describes a conversation he had with the American philosopher, Ingersoll. Now, Ingersoll was not only a confirmed agnostic but also a towering intellectual, a great scholar and an orator. He said to Swamiji, 'I believe in making the most of this world, in squeezing the orange dry, because this world is all that we are sure of.'

Swamiji said to him, 'I know a better way to squeeze the orange of this world, and I get more out of it! Think of the joy of loving man as God! Squeeze your orange this way and get ten thousand fold more out of it. Get every single drop!'

We too should benefit from Swamiji's wise counsel. We must squeeze the orange of the world for every last drop of happiness, with the love of God and the love of every man as God!

As Swami Vivekananda said:

> The nature of the soul is bliss, peace, unchanging. We have not to get it, we have it; only wash away the dross and see it.... Take a very high stand; knowing our universal nature, we must look with perfect calmness upon all the panorama of the world. It is but child's play, and we know that, so we cannot be disturbed by it.

How may we learn to look with perfect calmness upon life? How may we acquire the peaceful mind that ensures true happiness? How may we conquer irritation, annoyance and unhappiness?

2

The Four Rules of a Peaceful Life

There is an ancient story that tells us about a wise old man who was about to pass away. Knowing that he was on his deathbed, he called his four sons together and said to them, 'I do not have a great deal of money to pass on to you, but I do wish to teach you four golden rules of a peaceful life. If you build your life on these rules, you will be blessed with that which is the best of gifts—a peace-filled mind.'

The sons were eager to benefit from their father's wisdom and begged him to teach them this wonderful secret. The father gave them the four golden rules as promised. These were:

- Seek not to please men; seek only to please God
- Take serious things lightly, and light things seriously

- Laugh as much as you can
- Cultivate the spirit of acceptance

Seek Not to Please Men; Seek Only to Please God

The great musical genius and poet-saint of South India, Sri Tyagaraja was once ordered to attend the court of the Maratha king of Tanjore, Raja Sarfoji. The king had heard several of Tyagaraja's divine musical compositions, all of them addressed in profound devotion to Lord Sri Rama. The king was desirous that at least one such beautiful song should be composed in his honour too.

Poets and creative artists cannot be ordered to perform at the will and behest of ordinary mortals. Therefore, the king used the art of subtle temptation—he sent an emissary to the humble cottage of the poet-saint who was as poor as the proverbial church mouse—and tried to lure him with the bait of financial rewards.

The emissary used all the powers of persuasion at his command, to entice the saint to compose a song in praise of the king. He pointed out all the advantages of royal patronage; he gently reminded the saint of his utter poverty—the dilapidated state of the house, the shabby clothes he wore, the lowly food that he ate.

Sri Tyagaraja was adamant. 'This tongue was given to me to utter the name of the Lord. The seven notes on the musical scale were given to me that I might adore Him with my songs. How can I use them to sing the praise of an ordinary mortal?'

'But it is no ordinary mortal we are talking about,' protested the emissary. 'It is the ruler of the realm, the Raja who can wipe out your poverty by merely casting his glance on you!'

'That is as may be,' said the saint and he began to compose one of his most beautiful songs:

Nidhi sala sukhama
Ramuni sannidhi seva sukhama

Given below is a free translation of a few lines from this immortal *kriti:*

> What constitutes happiness? *Nidhi* (money) or Sri Rama's *Sannidhi* (divine presence)?
>
> What constitutes sweetness? A concoction of milk, butter, sugar and rice? Or the nectar of a bhajan of devotion to the Lord?
>
> What constitutes grace? A dip in the holy river Ganga of the soul? Or dabbling in the polluted waters of *nar-stuti* (the praise of an ordinary mortal)?

'Tell me the truth, oh my heart,' sang Sri Tyagaraja, 'What constitutes happiness? Money or Sri Rama's divine presence?'

His was a great soul that refused to be bought over by wealth. He sought to please God alone, and not men.

When we seek to please others, we often end up in defeat and bitterness. Trying to please others, we build up expectations; we imagine the rewards, the advantages and the appreciation that would accrue to us for our efforts and when this is not forthcoming, we end up blaming ourselves and others.

Have you heard the story of the foolish father and son who set out to sell their mule in the market? Father and son began to walk from their home, leading the mule by their side. As they went along, they met a neighbour who said, 'What fools you are! Here is a fat mule taking a pleasure walk and you two are huffing and puffing beside him! Why doesn't one of you ride the mule? He is a beast of burden after all and he must earn his keep. Go on, get up on the mule one of you. Let the mule sweat it out, why should you?'

Father and son looked at each other. 'He is right, son,' said the father. 'Our neighbour is a wise man. It is good that we should accept his counsel. I'll tell you what! You ride on the mule and I'll walk by your side.'

And so it was that the son climbed onto the back of the mule and they wended their way to the market. But before long, a stranger stopped them. Seizing the harness on the mule, he demanded of the son, 'Have you no respect for age? How could you allow your poor old father to trudge by your side while you are comfortably mounted on the mule like a petty tyrant? Have you no sense of decency or propriety? Get off that mule at once and let your father ride on it. As for you, a little exercise will do you good, so stretch those lazy limbs of yours!'

Taken aback by this outburst, the son hastily dismounted. He said to the father, 'See how people talk! We have to respect people's views or nobody will respect us in society. So let us do as this man says. You ride the mule and I will walk. That way, we will be free of blame.'

The father agreed and began to ride on the mule. 'We will reach the market soon,' he said to the son.

'The sooner we get rid of this beast, the better for us,' remarked the son. 'It has brought us nothing but trouble.'

A little while later, they were confronted by an old man who shouted, 'Stop! Stop!' at the top of his voice. Startled, they stopped at once and the old man began a tirade of abuse directed at the father. 'What kind of a father are you?' he demanded angrily. 'Is this poor boy your stepson that you treat him so shabbily? Don't you know that children are God's greatest gifts to us? How can you have the heart to ride on the mule like a nawab while the child who is your flesh and blood, walks wearily behind you? Get off that mule at once; shame on you!'

Father and son now gazed at each other in blank incomprehension. What could they do now? If both of them walked, they were called fools. If the son rode and the father walked, they called the son lazy. If the father rode and the son walked, they called the father heartless. Clearly, there was no pleasing some people!

They brooded on the unfairness of it all for a while and then they decided that they would both ride on the mule. That way, nobody would find fault with them.

The mule began to drag its feet as father and son sat on its back, poking and prodding it to move on. It was a weak and sickly mule to start with and the weight of two people proved too much for the poor beast. Hardly had he moved a few paces, when he began to bray pathetically.

An enraged man approached the struggling beast and pushed father and son off his back. 'You cruel, insensitive goons!' he yelled. 'Have you no compassion for this dumb and defenceless animal? How can you treat the poor animal so mercilessly? Get off, get off at once, I tell you!'

Now the father and the son were at the end of their tether. There was only one thing left for them to do, for all other options were exhausted. They got a stout pole and tied the mule upside down, suspended from the pole. They began to carry the pole between them, the mule suspended between them like a surrealist painting. They entered the market in this fashion and were greeted by jeers and catcalls. Never, ever had anyone come to the market carrying a mule on their shoulders!

You cannot please everyone. It is just not possible to please everyone. Therefore, don't try to please men but try to please God!

Many people live under constant stress, trying to 'keep up appearances' as the saying goes. 'What will the neighbours think if I walk to work?' 'What will my friends say if I don't treat them to a party?' 'What will the society say if I don't arrange a grand wedding reception for my daughter?' and so on.

I must confess I am amused, even amazed at this supposedly rhetorical question, *What will people say*! My answer is always this: Don't bother about what other people say! Let them say what they like. But do not let them upset you. What other people say does not really matter; it does not really count in the ultimate analysis. What really matters, what counts is what you do. Do your duty. Do whatever you have to do in the ever-radiant presence of the Lord. Seek only to please Him, seek not to please 'them', whoever they may be. Say to yourself again and again, 'They say...what do they say? Let them say!'

I am afraid many people live in a way that is basically aimed at pleasing or impressing others. Such a life will bring us no satisfaction. We will always be thinking of 'them' and 'others' and stop thinking about ourselves, or indeed, thinking for ourselves. This can lead to frustration and unhappiness.

Do not get carried away with judgements and opinions of people about you, be they praise or blame. Evaluate these judgements objectively in the light of your own judgement, in the light of your self-knowledge and accept whatever you consider to be appropriate.

Man, as they say, is a social animal. We live in society, and therefore, it is necessary that we observe certain norms and social obligations. It has rightly been said that there is nobody in the world who knows everything. It is equally true that we can learn something or the other from everyone we meet. By all means, respect views and attitudes of other people. Keep an open mind that is receptive to the ideas of other people but do not become a slave to their judgements.

Modern psychology emphasises that an individual should develop a healthy self-image. Ask yourself: Should your self-image be based on what others want, what others say and what others expect? Should others set the standards for where you live, how you live, which car you drive and what clothes you wear? Such a life would indeed be intolerable to any thinking person.

If you rely excessively on other people's praise and blame, you will develop a very poor sense of self-esteem. On the other hand, if you view yourself as a child of God, you will begin to feel good about yourself and realise that He created you with a definite purpose and plan which you alone can fulfil!

When you set out to please God, you will live up to your best potential. True, none of us is perfect. We have our share of weaknesses; we make mistakes. But we must not focus on these weaknesses; we must focus on God instead.

I heard a few years ago that many young women in the West were falling victim to an eating disorder called *anorexia nervosa*. In their anxiety to stay pencil-thin in imitation of models and film stars, they began to eat less and less, until they could not even stand the thought of food.

How sad it is when people are not comfortable with how they look, how they talk or how they walk! They are always comparing themselves unfavourably with others. They are constantly wishing that they could be different. 'If only I could be like her...' 'If I had his dress sense...' 'If I were as tall as you...' Such people are not happy with how God has made them! They do not like themselves and so they live by the likes and dislikes of others. They try to gain the approval of others; they try to please others in order to feel good about themselves.

Mr and Mrs Kapoor were celebrating their tenth wedding anniversary. 'It's your day today, honey,' Mr Kapoor said to his wife lovingly. 'We will go wherever you want and do whatever you want!'

'Do you really mean that?' Mrs Kapoor demanded. 'Will you take me wherever I want to go?'

'Sure, just state your wish and it shall be my command,' her husband assured her playfully.

'In that case,' she said, 'I would like to go to a five-star hotel for dinner tonight.'

Her kind and generous husband agreed. True, the outing was going to be very expensive, but after all it was their tenth anniversary. He would do his best, and more, to make his wife happy.

It was the first time that the couple was eating out at such a plush restaurant. The ambience, the decoration, the luxury of the place was indeed breathtaking. The waiters treated them like royalty. Mr Kapoor was really enjoying the experience.

However, Mrs Kapoor seemed to be labouring under considerable stress. She constantly kept looking over her shoulder. Every time the door opened and someone entered the restaurant, she would almost jump out of her skin and scan their faces eagerly. While her husband was thoroughly enjoying the delicious and expensive dishes placed before them, she was hardly aware of what she ate.

The lavish meal came to an end. 'It's the best ice cream that I have ever had,' Mr Kapoor exclaimed with satisfaction, as he paid the bill, adding a generous tip for the waiter. 'In fact, it's the best meal I've ever had, don't you agree, honey? I must thank you for making this experience possible. After all, it was your decision to come here.'

Mrs Kapoor was looking dejected and downcast. It looked as if she would burst into tears any moment. 'What's the matter, dear?' enquired Mr Kapoor anxiously. 'Is it that the food wasn't to your taste? Why, you look ill! Are you sure you are alright?'

Mrs Kapoor was trying to blink back her tears. 'It's so unfair,' she told him with a low sob. 'We've spent ten thousand rupees to eat at this place and none of our friends have seen us here! Of what use is it, if they don't know we are dining at a five-star restaurant? What a waste the whole thing is!'

This is what living by others' standards can do to you. You end up living a life of pretence and hypocrisy. You are wearing a mask, you put on a face or an attitude to impress other people, and you cease to be true to yourself.

A holy man of God was once invited by a wealthy merchant to have lunch at his new house. When the saint arrived at the gates of the palatial residence, he was driven away by the guards who thought he was a beggar.

A few minutes later, the holy man returned, wrapped in an expensive silk and gold shawl. This attire gained him instant admittance into the merchant's house.

'Your servants would not let me enter the house when I came in my ochre robes,' the saint remarked to the merchant. 'That is only natural, Swamiji,' said the merchant smugly. 'The elite of the town are present here today, and it is entirely proper that they should see you at your best! Now they know that you are a force to reckon with, a grand, impressive figure in that resplendent shawl!'

The saint smiled and did not utter a word in reply.

When they were seated at the table, a grand feast was laid before them. The wealthy guests began to eat hastily. They did not want to miss out on any of the scrumptious dishes offered to them.

As for the saint, he quietly took away the shawl that covered him. Underneath, he still wore his ochre robes. He laid the shawl on the table and began to put food on it. Hot steaming vegetables, creamy kheer, fragrant rice, soft rotis, luscious mithai and desserts—everything was heaped onto the shawl!

'Swamiji!' thundered his host, red-faced with anger. 'What are you doing?'

'My friend, I realise that I am not the guest you invited to dine with you,' the saint replied. 'When I came in my humble attire, I was refused admittance. It is this shawl which made you welcome me and seat me at this table with your honoured guests. And so, it is this shawl which is your guest, and it is this shawl which should be the real recipient of your lavish hospitality. As for the real me in my poor ochre robes, I do not deserve to eat anything at your grand feast!'

Let us not try to pretend to be someone else. You do not need people's praise and approval when you do what God wants you to do!

When the famous American music composer Gershwin was a struggling, young musician, he was interviewed for the post of assistant to the illustrious Irving Berlin, who was then the top musician in Broadway. Berlin saw the young man's potential and told him, 'I can offer you the job of my assistant and you will be paid thrice as much as you are earning now. But you will end up as a second-rate version of Irving Berlin. But if you struggle in your present position and work hard on your style, you will turn out to be a master in the future! My advice to you is to be yourself.'

Gershwin accepted the older man's wise counsel and Berlin's prophecy came to be true!

God wants us to be true to ourselves and our own nature. He does not want us to become clones who imitate others.

Take Serious Things Lightly, and Light Things Seriously!

Have you heard the beautiful song which begins with the words:

Little drops of water, little grains of sand,
Make the mighty ocean and the pleasant land!

It is the little things of life that count! But sadly, in our mad rush for bigger and greater things, we ignore those little things that make life truly meaningful.

Look at the huge banyan tree which spreads its leafy green branches so wide that dozens of people can rest comfortably under its shade. Do you realise that it came from a tiny seed? Let us take care of the little things of life and it is out of these little habits that our life is shaped.

There is an amusing story about a king who built a magnificent temple of Lord Shiva. On the day of the consecration, he had arranged for a grand ritual of worship. So, he ordered every citizen in the kingdom to bring one jug of milk and pour it into the temple's tank. This was to be done on the previous night so that the worship could start early in the morning.

Now, the citizens of the kingdom said to themselves, 'Everyone is bringing one jug of milk. Who would know the difference if I took a jug of water instead? A little water would hardly make a difference in a tank full of milk!'

And so, under cover of darkness, everyone brought a jug of water and poured it into the tank, confident that no one would notice anything amiss. The next morning, it was discovered that the tank was filled with water. Not a single person had thought it his duty to offer a little milk for the Lord's special puja!

Everyone matters. Every little bit counts. I am sure you have all heard of the conundrum given below:

> Something important had to be done urgently. Everybody thought somebody will do it. So nobody did it. Anybody could have done it, but it was not done because nobody thought of doing it himself.

Little things matter, and very often, so do little people! Do you know the height of Napoleon Bonaparte? He was barely 5'1". As for Julius Caesar, he was just one inch taller, at 5'2". Arrogant Britishers described Mahatma Gandhi as 'that short, toothless person', 'the half-naked fakir'. But this same short, toothless, half-naked fakir shook the mighty British Empire to its very roots!

Take light things seriously! Small things, small tasks are as important as the great things of life. A perfectionist is one who pays as much attention to small details as to great tasks. Such a person peels an orange with as much care as he implements an important project. This is also the teaching of karma yoga, which does not distinguish between 'low' and 'high' work in the execution of one's duty.

Take serious things lightly! Do not raise a storm in a teacup over trifling issues. It is only our inflated egos that goad us into taking offence over every petty issue.

Sometime ago, I read of a Union minister who decided to take a flight to his destination. As this was done at the eleventh hour, the minister could not be accommodated in the First Class section which was already filled with passengers who had paid the full fare. The minister, who was getting a free ride, kept the flight waiting. When he saw that there was no vacancy in First Class, he began to throw tantrums and even threatened the flight crew with violent threats of dismissal. In his egotistical arrogance, he imagined that he could bully anyone and everyone into doing what he wanted. He thought too highly of himself—how could he, a minister, travel in the economy class with lesser mortals!

As it happened, there was a journalist on the same flight who recorded all that was happening. When the event was reported in the media the next day, the minister's action was loudly condemned by everyone, and he was eventually forced to apologise for his disgraceful conduct.

Alas, many of us develop inflated egos and actually begin to believe that the world functions only because of us. But this is far from true. None of us is indispensable.

When you eliminate the ego, you will grow in the realisation that all of us are equal in the eyes of God. Truly, great men grow in humility as they evolve in stature. On the other hand, men who flaunt their wealth, power and possessions only reveal their immaturity.

There was a king who decided to build an impressive marble temple to commemorate his victory over his enemies. He ordered that no expenses should be spared to make the temple the biggest, best and most impressive structure in the kingdom. Thousands of labourers were drafted, and the best marble was brought from the farthest corners of the kingdom. Hundreds of horses and oxen were brought in to transport the heavy marble slabs to the construction site.

A poor old woman lived in a dilapidated cottage on the way to the temple. She was thrilled to hear that a house of God was to come up near her own humble house. She, too, had heard of the grand plans of the king for the temple, and prayed that she be alive to see the wonderful temple completed. She longed to contribute in some way or the other, but she was so poor that she could hardly spare a copper coin.

Every day horses and oxen passed before her hut, carrying heavy marble slabs. Taking pity on the poor animals, she drew a little straw out of her worn mattress and offered it to the beasts that stopped before her door. The animals gratefully chewed on the straw and cast such a loving glance at her that her heart was indeed touched. Soon, she made it a habit to offer a little straw to all the beasts pausing by her door.

By the time the temple was constructed, her old mattress had become threadbare. But she was delighted that she had done her mite for the Lord, and for the dumb and defenceless creatures who were her brothers and sisters in the united divine family of creation. 'I do not have much to offer to the Lord,' she said to herself. 'But I'm glad I offered what little I could.'

On the day that the temple was to be consecrated, the king had a vision of the Lord. The Lord told him, 'The honours of the first puja in my temple should be offered to the poor old woman who dwells in the dilapidated cottage to the east of the temple for it is she who has offered what is dear to me.'

And so it came to pass, that the poor old lady who offered a little straw to the oxen and horses, was recognised by the Lord as His chosen one!

Once, there was a little boy who showed great interest in music. His mother arranged for him to take piano lessons. When the famous Polish pianist, Jan Paderewski, came to their city for a concert, the mother decided to take her son to the concert so that the little boy could draw inspiration from the Master.

They arrived early and found their seats. Spotting a friend in the audience, the mother went up to greet him. Left alone, the little boy decided to explore the grand auditorium and wandered off on his own. Finding a door ajar in a corner, he walked through, unaware of the red letters above the entrance which carried the warning: No Admittance.

When the lights dimmed and the concert was about to begin, the mother returned to her seat and was horrified to find her little boy missing. Imagine her shock when she saw the velvet curtains parting to reveal the stage, where her son was seated before the magnificent Steinway piano, strumming the keys of the only tune he knew, *Twinkle, twinkle little star*.

The audience gazed in wonder at the strange sight before them when the spotlight focussed on Paderewski who made his entrance on stage. At a glance, the master understood the situation. He quickly moved to the piano and whispered in the little boy's ear, 'Just keep on playing, son! You're doing wonderfully well!'

The little boy smiled and continued to play the familiar tune, blissfully unaware that a thousand pairs of eyes were staring at him in disbelief. Leaning over, Paderewski began playing the bass part with his left hand.

The youngster was delighted at the beautiful music emanating from the piano. With a radiant smile, he focussed on the keys before him, playing the tune with great care.

Soon, Paderewski brought his right hand around the other side of the young pianist and added a running obligato to the simple tune. The novice and the great master had transformed what could have been a potentially embarrassing situation into a wonderful, triumphant creative experience. The audience was transported by the music and gave a standing ovation at the end of this marvellous rendition.

Paderewski was indeed a grand master, who took the serious lapse on the stage in his stride. He had respected the enthusiasm of the little boy and taken his playful effort seriously! What started off as a mistake had been turned into a miracle!

Take light things seriously! Do everything in the spirit of offering to the Lord. It does not matter how lowly your station may be; it does not matter how humble the task you perform.

It was Martin Luther King who said:

> If a man is called to be a street sweeper, he should sweep streets even as Michelangelo painted, or Beethoven played music, or Shakespeare wrote poetry. He should sweep streets so well that all the hosts of heaven and earth will pause to say, 'Here lived a great sweeper who did his job well.'

Unfortunately, many of us are prone to equate 'greatness' with fame, fortune and power. However, true perfection consists in the way we attend to the little details of life. Therefore, we must concentrate on the task before us, the task at hand.

A man came to the Buddha and asked him, 'Are you the Messiah?'

'No,' answered the Buddha.

'Are you a saint, then?' the man wanted to know.

'No,' was the reply.

'Then surely, you must be a teacher,' the man proclaimed.

Again, the same answer. 'No.'

'What are you then?' demanded the man impatiently.

'I am awake,' the Buddha answered.

He was expressing a great spiritual truth in those simple words. For the goal of all spiritual practices is simply to awaken. The great ones of this earth—wise, loving, evolved souls, are no different from the rest of us. They simply recognise and remember who they are. This is why the most enlightened teachers tell you that they are your fellow pilgrims, fellow seekers on the path.

There was a spiritual seeker, Jignasu, who was told about a holy man, a sage who lived on a lonely, remote mountaintop. It was believed that this wise man had an answer for every question, a solution to every problem. Merely by spending a few minutes in his presence, one's life would be changed forever.

Naturally, the seeker was anxious to meet such an evolved soul.

'If only I could just see him,' he said to himself, 'I would count myself blessed! If only I could share a few seconds with him, I would feel truly enlightened!'

He decided to set out in search of the sage's abode. For days together, he walked across hills, rivers, valleys and streams to locate the mountain where the great guru lived. After a tough and exhausting climb, he finally arrived at the sage's front door.

Trembling with intense emotional excitement, he knocked at the door. It was opened by a lowly man in poor clothes whom he took to be a servant. The servant greeted him and led him through the house. They passed through several corridors and rooms, and the servant kept on talking as they walked. However, the seeker's mind was so fixed on the experience ahead of him, that he hardly paid any attention to what the man was saying. The servant glanced at him as he talked and finally, they both arrived at a locked door. He opened the door which led on to the backyard. Wordlessly, he indicated that the visitor should leave the house.

'But I've come all the way to meet the guru,' the seeker protested. 'I must have at least a few minutes with him!'

'You just did,' answered the sage, as he let the man out and shut the door firmly.

We are so preoccupied with 'big' issues that we have no time to spare for the here and the now. Our answers, the solutions to our problems are not always to be found on a mountaintop; they may be staring you in the face right where you are!

Some people, unfortunately, become permanent, professional 'seekers'. They are reading books, pondering deep questions, attending seminars and conferences on philosophy and spirituality and engaging in a lifelong quest. They forget that God can speak to them through the ordinary people they meet, through the grass, the flowers, the sun, the moon and the stars. They fail to realise that His ways are indeed mysterious, and that He can express Himself through the touch of a friend or the smile of a loved one or the shining eyes of a child.

Your mukti, your liberation, your salvation does not necessarily come from the hands of a powerful, impressive, authoritative figure. It can come to you through humble people whom you meet in the byways of life.

Many of us imagine God as a sort of the Old Testament figure—in long, flowing robes and a white beard, seated on a cloud, hurling lightning and thunderbolts at the sinful world. But God lives within you, in the temple of your heart; He speaks to you in silence; He speaks to you through your intuitions, visions and dreams! Every person you meet is a manifestation of God. Every creature that breathes the breath of life is an aspect of the Maker. Each and every one of them can teach you valuable lessons in a new, unexpected and unique way! Therefore, the Lord is described as *Deenabandhu* and *Deenanath*. He is the friend, the brother of the humble and the lowly. When we take them seriously, we will surely find the answers we are seeking.

So take serious things lightly! Whenever the great inventor, Thomas Alva Edison felt lost and helpless and found it impossible to proceed with a difficult experiment, he would adopt a unique way out of the stressful situation. He would go to sleep on a couch holding tightly on to a rock in his hand. As he dozed, he would dip into his subconscious mind, where he knew the answer to his problems would be found. As he slipped into sleep, his hold on the rock would be loosened and it would fall down with a thud. The noise would awaken Edison and he would spring up, awake and alert—the solution to his problem now available to him. He would quickly write it down and proceed with his interrupted experiment.

The noise, shout and shows of the world often distract us from the inner spirit, with its vast and deep store of wisdom. This inner genius can be tapped through deep relaxation. A good night's sleep, or a relaxing short nap will clear the cobwebs of your mind, and allow your inner wisdom to shine forth.

We often dismiss the 'little' people and events of our lives. We take our friends and family members for granted. By doing so, we simply overlook their special gifts and insights. It has been said that every person who walks the earth is a God in disguise. We celebrate a few great souls and extol them as leaders, but what we must do is lift our vision and find the highest in those around us.

People seek fame and fortune in the world outside, as they believe that if they become rich and famous, they will also be happy and content. They have got their notions slightly mixed up. If they do what makes them truly happy, appreciation and contentment will naturally follow.

After his life-changing experience in Walden, American thinker and philosopher, Henry David Thoreau went to visit his friend and fellow intellectual, Emerson. He told Emerson all about his experience, living in the woods.

'What would you say is the most important lesson you learnt at Walden?' Emerson enquired of him.

Thoreau answered emphatically, 'Simplify, simplify, simplify!'

Emerson smiled and responded, 'I think one "simplify" would have done quite well!'

In a beautiful book called *Wisdom of the Heart*, bestselling author Alan Cohen tells us:

> The lighter we get, the higher we soar…we gain freedom in releasing possessions…and begin to appreciate the simple things of life…we recognise that simplicity is the flower that brings the intellect to its knees and recognises the greatest riches of all.

Laugh As Much As You Can!

I am convinced that many of our problems can be solved, if only we relearn the gift of laughter. The tragedy of modern man is that he does not laugh enough. Laughter, I always say, is a powerful tonic. It vitalises the body, mind and spirit. It is an excellent dry-cleaner—it cleanses you from inside.

There is something funny about all of us, sometimes ridiculous, sometimes even absurd! Each one of us has his faults and failings, his quirks and oddities. So learn to laugh at yourself first. When you learn to laugh at yourself, you will never be offended when others laugh at you. For that you need to stop taking yourself too seriously.

There was a famous orator who was invited to lecture at the Dublin University Hall in Ireland. On the day that his public lecture was scheduled, it rained very heavily in Dublin. Many people stayed away and the auditorium was practically empty.

Naturally, the orator was upset. When he began his lecture, he cast a sour glance at the scattered audience and said to them, 'Do you know that I am a famous orator? I have addressed large audiences at international conferences, at the UNO and at the House of Commons. I am also a famous playwright, a distinguished thinker, a luminous intellectual...' and he went on and on with the list of his achievements. He ended it all by saying, 'But the pity of it all is that I am so many and you are so few!'

Do you know that there is a very popular movement called the Laughter Club which is spreading rapidly all over the world? Its founders believe that 'laughter has no language, knows no boundaries and does not discriminate between caste, creed and colour. It is a powerful emotion and has all the ingredients for uniting the entire world'.

I could not agree more! Truly has it been said: Laugh, and the world laughs with you!

The holistic benefits of laughter have been well-researched and well-documented. Laughter relaxes the muscles, expands the blood vessels, improves circulation and reduces the level of stress-causing hormones. Above all, laughter exercises your facial muscles improving your face value!

It has been calculated that it takes forty-two muscles to frown and a scowl causes lines and wrinkles to form on your skin. Whereas, you use just seventeen muscles to smile and it reduces wrinkles and tightens your chin and makes you look younger. So what will you choose—a scowl or a smile?

It was Victor Hugo who said, 'Laughter is the sun that drives the winter from the human face'. When you feel sad, depressed, tense, just look at your face in a mirror. It seems so serious, so constricted, so tight, that you will not want others to see it! The stress and strain reflected on your face is obviously due to negative emotions that are playing havoc inside you.

Cheerfulness is the new wonder drug. Doctors tell us that our blood molecules contain receptors which receive signals from the brain. When you are happy, cheerful and contented, the receptors transmit these signals of happiness and the healing process within you is accelerated. Indeed, modern medicine assures us that if we laugh more, we grow healthier. Many doctors are convinced that if a man is happy and light-hearted, disease will not draw close to him and even if it does, it will not stay with him for long.

Did you know that many of the great icons of humanity were also lovers of laughter? Socrates, St Francis of Assisi, St Teresa of Ávila, Sri Ramakrishna Paramahansa, Sri Ramana Maharshi, Papa Ramdas, Mahatma Gandhi and Sadhu Vaswani, to name but a few. All of them possessed a wonderful sense of humour.

Mahatma Gandhi said, 'If I didn't have a sense of humour, I would have committed suicide long ago!'

Papa Ramdas said, 'I did not have to shed tears. I laughed my way to God.'

Sadhu Vaswani had a sparkling sense of humour. He could sometimes make us burst out in laughter. I remember one day, a doctor-friend who thought very highly of himself, came to him and said, 'I have decided to give up my practice and devote all my time to the service of the country.'

Sadhu Vaswani said to us, 'I am not sure if he has given up his practice or his practice has given him up!'

People sometimes ask me very solemnly, 'Dada, does God ever laugh?'

My answer to them is, 'Yes, God does laugh! He does not laugh at our weaknesses or imperfections, our heartaches and failures. But He does laugh at the ungodly world which thinks it can efface God out of existence.'

God also laughs when some of us remark that they can teach God how to make a better world. I find it amusing that many people swear that they wish to serve God but they all want to serve Him in an advisory capacity!

There is a wealthy woman I know who rejoices in saying, 'I wish God made me His secretary. I would teach Him how to make the world better and happier!'

God laughs too, when two brothers quarrel over the land and say to each other, 'This land is mine and that is yours'. God laughs for He knows that everything belongs to Mother Earth.

When the great Italian leader, Garibaldi, was shot in the neck and critically wounded, one of his companions asked him if he had a last message for his mother. 'Yes,' said Garibaldi, weak with losing much blood, but still managing to grin. 'Tell her I will live to be seventy-six!'

One morning, it began to rain heavily as William Dean Howells and Mark Twain came out of church after the Sunday service.

Howells gazed at the sky anxiously and asked his friend, 'Do you think it will stop?'

'It always has,' was Mark Twain's simple reply.

William Thackeray wrote in his masterpiece, *Vanity Fair*:

> The world is a glass, and gives back to every man the reflection of his own face. Frown at it, and it will in turn, look lowly upon you. Laugh at it and with it, and it is a jolly, kind companion.

A nervous, young journalist was given the prestigious assignment of interviewing HG Wells. All the way to the hotel he was staying at, she rehearsed how she would greet him, how she would introduce herself and shake his hand warmly.

As she knocked at the door of his room, she felt her nerves fail. A bright, cheerful face with dancing eyes greeted her.

'Good morning...hello...' she stammered. 'I'm glad to meet you and I am HG Wells!' and she froze with horror at her absurd blunder.

HG Wells smiled beatifically. 'How remarkable,' he said casually, 'I say, even our initials are the same. Do come in!'

I am told that laughter has indeed become a 'serious' business these days! Laughter Workshops and Laughter Leader Training programmes are being held all over the world. People are also being taught 'the underlying philosophy' and the 'skills' of different kinds of laughter.

My advice to you is, 'With or without the theory, learn to laugh! Laugh at yourself. Laugh with others. Laugh your way to health and harmony!'

Here is what Sri Anandamayi Ma tells us:

> Whenever you have the chance, laugh as much as you can. By this, all the rigid knots in your body will be loosened. But to laugh superficially is not enough; your whole being must be united in laughter, both outwardly and inwardly...what you usually do is laugh with your mouth, while your mind and emotions are not involved. You must laugh with your whole countenance, with your whole heart and soul, with all the breath of your life...you will then see how the laughter that flows from such a heart defeats the world!

The Jews have had a tragic history for the last two thousand years or more. But they have been blessed with a lovely sense of humour.

People often ask Israelis why the Good Lord selected them for such large calamities. The reply is in the form of a hilarious story which all of us can relate to!

A poor man was forced to carry an unbearable load on his back. One day, he dropped his load in great anguish and cried out heart-rendingly, 'Oh death! Come and free me from this misery!'

In a flash, the Angel of Death was at his side, enquiring politely, 'You called for me?'

'Yes,' said the poor man, quickly pulling himself together, 'please help me put this load back upon my shoulders, would you?'

This oppressed community has always borne its burden with laughter, and the faith given to them by Abraham, Jacob and Moses.

There was a rabbi who prayed daily, for hours together. He lived in the abiding conviction that his prayers would be answered. After one such arduous prayer session, his sceptical wife asked him, 'And what did you pray for today?'

'I prayed that the rich should give alms to the poor,' he replied.

'And do you think the Good Lord heard your prayer?' she enquired sarcastically.

Strong in his faith, the rabbi replied, 'I'm sure He heard at least half of it, because the poor have agreed to accept what the rich give to them.'

This is the miracle element in enduring faith—a man can laugh at himself in the most trying circumstances.

A Jew was found lying across the railroad tracks, with a loaf of bread tucked under his arm. A policeman rushed up to him and demanded, 'Hey, what do you think you are doing?'

'I've had enough,' said the man stoically. 'I don't wish to live any longer. I'm waiting for the train to run over me.'

'But why are you carrying that loaf of bread?' the policeman wanted to know.

'The way the trains run here,' sighed the would-be suicide victim, 'you could starve to death, waiting for one.'

Laughter, especially the ability to laugh at oneself, is the greatest gift we can have. For humour tempers our faith, even as carbon tempers iron, to produce a tougher, more resistant substance.

Cultivate the Spirit of Acceptance!

Make this the mantra of your life: 'Yes Father, yes and always yes!'

Many people come to me and complain, 'You advocate the philosophy of acceptance, but don't you think it will make people lethargic and lazy?'

I beg to differ with them on this point. I do not think people will become lazy and lethargic if they follow the philosophy of acceptance. I believe it is a dynamic concept which encourages us to do our very best, to put forth our best efforts to achieve what we desire. But if we cannot achieve those results, you must accept it as the will of God, in the faith that there must be some good in it. As I always say, there is a meaning of mercy in all the incidents and accidents of life. Therefore let us accept everything with the mantra, 'Yes Father, yes and always yes!'

There is a meaning of mercy in all that happens to us for God is all love and all wisdom. He is too loving to punish us. He is too wise to make a mistake. Therefore, if something comes to us that is contrary to our personal will, we must accept it as the will of God.

Sadhu Vaswani always taught us, 'Every disappointment is His appointment'. The problems and difficulties that we face in life are sent to us with a definite purpose. We can always derive benefit and wisdom from the most unpleasant experiences. This is why enlightened souls have always expressed gratitude to God in trying times. It was Dale Carnegie who said, 'When we have accepted the worst, we have nothing more to lose. And that automatically means we have everything to gain.'

It is not possible for us, with our limited intelligence, to explain everything that happens in life. Why do I have to struggle while others succeed effortlessly? Why do I have to face so many disappointments? You can analyse and speculate by all means but the important thing for you is to accept, to take life as it comes and get on with it. It was a wise man who said: 'Acceptance is not submission; it is acknowledgement of the facts of the situation'.

When you wish to take on the challenges of life, ask yourself first: What is the worst that can happen to me? The secret of facing life's challenges is to be prepared for the worst and to hope for the best! Anything in life that we refuse to accept will only impede our progress and constantly irritate us, until we learn to make peace with it.

The Irish dramatist, JM Synge, gave us a beautiful play called *Riders to the Sea.* It tells us of an old Irish woman who loses her husband and all her seven sons one after another. She accepts her loss with fortitude and at the end of the play, when her only remaining son is to be buried, she utters the moving prayer: 'God, Thou gavest. Thou hast taken away. Blessed be Thy Name!'

By accepting the worst the mother finds release and liberation from sorrow.

Sometime ago, one of the sisters of our Sadhu Vaswani satsang came to see me. She was in great emotional distress and could not keep back her tears as she spoke to me.

Her husband, a kind and devoted man whom she loved dearly, had been posted abroad. She could not accompany him for his organisation did not permit the families to join employees on such an assignment for technical reasons.

'I don't want him to leave me and go abroad,' she said. I told her, 'Ask him to give up his job or pray that this assignment gets cancelled.'

Perhaps my answer might have appeared cruel to her at that time. 'I do not pray for this or that to happen,' I said to her. 'I shall pray instead that you have an understanding of what God wills for you, and that you may cooperate with His will and let it work uninterrupted, in and through you!'

When her husband went on his assignment, she bade him a tearful farewell. Her face clouded with grief, she told me, 'You did not do anything for me. You could have helped me if only you wished to do so!'

I smiled and said to her, 'Sister, do not despair! God fulfils Himself in many ways.'

After a few months, I had the opportunity to meet her again. She was indeed a transformed creature! Her face was wreathed in smiles. She was as joyous as a child with a new toy.

'Thank you, Dada!' she exclaimed. 'Now I do know what you meant, there is the hand of divine love and wisdom in all that happens. When my husband departed, I was utterly inconsolable. Then, gradually I thought of what you said: If God had willed my dear one to travel to a faraway land, it must also be for my good. And indeed, it has proved to be so. Now that I am alone at home, I have a lot of time to spare. I utilise it to study the Gita, the Guru Granth Sahib and Sadhu Vaswani's books on the *Sant bani* and the lives of saints—something that I have always wanted to do and never had the time for! I pray and meditate as often as I can. I attend the satsang every day. I sing God's name and I serve the children of the poor and the lowly. And I feel so happy and blessed!'

The philosophy of wise acceptance had turned her into a radiant soul!

3

The Life of Modern Man

Here is a thought-provoking passage sent to me by a sister in the US. She tells me, she found it on the internet:

> The paradox of our times is that we have taller buildings, but shorter tempers; wider freeways, but narrower viewpoints; we spend more, but have less; we buy more, but enjoy less; we have more degrees, but less sense; more medicines, but less wellness; we have conquered outer space, but not inner space; we have cleaned up the air, but polluted the soul; we have split the atom, but not our prejudices; we have become long on quantity, but short on quality; we live in fancier houses, but broken homes...

Today, we can fly in the air like birds, swim in the sea like fish, but alas, we do not know how to live on earth like men! In short, we have made tremendous progress, made several path-breaking discoveries, but somewhere in the process, we seem to have lost ourselves!

Truly has it been said that modern man is so busy earning a living that he has no time left to live!

Fast, faster, fastest! We want everything instantly. We have fast food, fast cars, instant messaging, non-stop flights, speed dialling—short cuts for everything. We beat the red signal at traffic lights; we overtake others at great risk to ourselves; we simply cannot bear to wait.

Where is all this hurry taking us? Why are we hurtling at such a breakneck speed?

I must remind you of one of the golden proverbs which characterised life in the good old days: *Slow and steady wins the race.*

I wonder how many of you believe in its efficacy, wisdom and sound sense.

A Victorian poet talks about life in the pre-industrial age, which 'ran gaily, like the sparkling Thames'. Poets have always compared the passage of life to the flow of the river—gently, steadily, tirelessly, the stream flows on and on.

You only have to think of rivers today to realise that the metaphor will not hold good any longer! Our rivers no longer run clear and steady. They are muddied, polluted, poisoned by chemicals and industrial effluents. Often they are in spate, overflowing their banks, causing enormous tragedies with loss of numerous lives and damage to property.

We are hurtling through life at maddening speed. Our favourite 'rides' are roller coasters on which people pay money to climb and then scream in fear as they are hurtled through loops and falls and steep drops! What are we looking for? What do we hope to find in such breathtaking pastimes?

Slow and steady, this was the pace of life, even fifty years ago and this was how men and women, old and young lived their lives.

The ubiquitous 'instant' mode has entered our personal and professional lives too, and we pay the price with stress, tension, neurosis and unheard physical ailments. Experts say human nerves are unable to withstand the stress and strain associated with modern life.

Rush, rush, rush! Executives are jet-setting across the globe. Visiting customers in Nigeria today, meeting with bankers in London tomorrow, trade conferences in Buenos Aires the day after, off to Chicago for a new collaboration afterwards…

Go, go, go! Tiny tots in primary schools go for swimming lessons before school, tennis practice after and computer classes in the late evening…

Hurry, hurry, hurry! Mothers are virtually on roller skates, dropping off their children at school, heading to work themselves, attending meetings, calling on doctors and bankers and plumbers and electricians, attending to household chores and managing servants amid all this…

In days gone by, we did everything in a relaxed and leisurely manner. We walked to the school, to the park and to the library. We spent hours poring over books. We played long, refreshing games, indoors and outdoors. We prayed together, laughed and talked together as extended families. Uncles and aunts visited us and were our honoured and cherished guests, sometimes staying back at our houses for days.

You will not believe me when I say this: We had time for everything those days. We had time for people; we had time to listen to others; we had time to devote to meaningful activities and time for relaxation and hobbies. And yet, we had the same twenty-four hours per day as you have now!

I have met men who are so busy with their work that they have no time to give to their children and families.

I have heard children say that they are so loaded with schoolwork that they don't have time to play!

I have heard housewives complain that they are virtually run off their feet with their multiple chores, so much so that they can't even have a moment to themselves.

Nowadays, many young men and women in India work in what are called 'sunrise' industries—boom industries like BPOs, and such is the nature of their jobs that they never get to see the sunrise! They work from 11 pm to 8 am; they sleep from 10 am to 6 pm. So, they miss out on the sunset too! And they get back to work when the rest of the world falls asleep.

Professors and psychologists are deeply disturbed by the lifestyle of these young people, which is so hectic that it verges on the unhealthy.

The greatest malady of modern life is that man permanently seems to be on a treadmill. He is on the move all the time, running, running, running and still in the same place!

Many of my friends tell me that they can't find five minutes in their day, for the practice of daily silence or for a brief period of quiet meditation.

However, almost everyone does find time for one or two hours before the TV, perhaps the world's favourite entertainment medium today. And what do they watch? Action, violence, murder and disasters. Even the daily news is not free from these elements.

I am told that engineers and technocrats working in certain industries are turning deaf due to the decibel levels of the machinery. Equally, young women who are constantly talking on their cell phones are also suffering from undue problems of the ear, including earaches and infections.

What price do we pay for wealth and progress?

Under these circumstances, is it at all surprising that we are constantly prone to irritation, annoyance and unhappiness?

The Buddha identified desire as the main cause of human suffering. However, he also taught us that this suffering could be ended by what he called *right living.* The essence of this is what the Buddhists call the *Middle Path*, i.e. avoiding extremes.

The ancient philosopher, Plotinus, advised us thus:

> Withdraw into yourself and look. And if you do not find yourself beautiful as yet, do as does the creator of the statue that is to be made beautiful: He cuts away here, he smoothens there, he makes this line lighter, this other purer, until the face of the statue becomes beautiful. So do you also! Cut away all that is excessive; straighten all that is crooked; bring light to all that is shadowed; labour to make all glow with beauty, and do not cease chiselling on your statue, until there shall shine on you the splendour of virtue!

When Nakulapita, who was old, weak and ailing, came to the Master for solace and comfort, the Buddha told him, 'True it is that you are weak and ailing. For a person carrying this body about, to claim but a moment's health would be foolish. For this reason, thus, you should train yourself: "Though my body is sick, my mind should not be sick". Thus, must you train yourself.'

Mindfulness is the key to peace and joy. The tremendous physical and material progress that man has made is of no value to him, unless he cultivates the right attitude of mind. It is this that will bring him peace and joy.

4

Irritation and Annoyance are Now All-pervasive

When we say 'irritation' or 'annoyance', we always associate these terms with trifles, petty issues, events and situations that are full of what we call 'nuisance value'. So you might ask, why do we have to take irritation and annoyance so seriously? Have we not agreed that they are, after all, trifling and petty?

A middle-aged housewife was asked to list all the things and events that added to her list of everyday irritations. She wrote down the following list:

- Ringing of the morning alarm just when she is sinking into a deep and a dreamless sleep
- Waking up family members, one after the other, running around to get them ready for school/college/work/business

- Constant ringing of the telephone/doorbell
- Dealing with maidservants and the provocations they bring
- Waiting interminably for the bus/public transport
- Carrying a load of shopping bags home
- Cooking breakfasts/lunches/dinners and other meals day after day after day

Taken individually, these are no doubt trifles. But taken collectively, they represent continuous little snips and cuts which will eventually make one's peace of mind and serenity wear thin. Minor or superficial they may be but they undermine your effectiveness and add raw, sharp edges to your personality. Before long, you begin to snap and lose your temper with your near and dear ones, and the petty annoyance you started with becomes a veritable contagion! Our capacity for patience and tolerance is torn to shreds; serenity and calm fly away from us.

When major crises and tough trials loom over us, we tend to tackle them with great courage, fortitude and resourcefulness. But when trifling irritations and constant frustrations bother, we tend to lose our cool.

I am told that the great Victorian writer, Thomas Carlyle, who has written masterpieces like *The French Revolution* and *Of Heroes and Hero Worship*, was given to the habit of writing into the late hours of night. He would often go to bed well past midnight. Naturally, he liked to sleep late. However, this became a problem when his neighbour bought a rooster. Roosters, as we all know, are nature's own morning alarm service. They begin to crow early in the morning and they crow loudly enough to wake the neighbourhood. The early crowing of the rooster so vexed Carlyle that he confronted his neighbour angrily one day.

Taken aback by his vehemence, the neighbour protested, 'Don't tell me the harmless crowing of a rooster bothers you so much!'

Carlyle replied, 'No, it's not just the crowing of the rooster that bothers me. It's lying there waiting for him to crow!'

There was a professor in college, who had problems with a very lively and spirited class, and she had great difficulty in controlling them. She thought of them as problem-students and troublemakers, but they loved and respected her because they believed she gave them freedom to be themselves in class.

When the end of the academic year approached, a bunch of the most lively and talkative students came to see her, before her last scheduled lecture for that term.

'What do you want?' she asked them curtly.

'Ma'am, you know we will be attending your last lecture tomorrow...' began the class representative.

The Professor turned her fury on them. 'Yes, thank God for that! I've just about had enough of you and I hope I'll never ever have to see any of you again because yours is one of the worst classes I've had the misfortune to teach. I will be happy to see the last of the whole bunch of you!'

The class representative and his friends stood still for a minute, their shock visible on their young faces. Then, the representative said, 'I'm sorry we made you feel that way, Ma'am, do forgive us.'

They left quietly. In their hands they carried a beautiful hand-made card in which each one of the students in the class had signed their names. The card read: To the Wonderful Teacher who allowed us to be ourselves and encouraged our creativity—with deep gratitude from the MBA batch of 2002.

The teacher lost a wonderful opportunity to realise how much the students appreciated her. As for the students, they were disappointed and disillusioned to realise that their favourite teacher harboured such ill-feelings about them.

Meena was a hard-working, efficient, smart and ambitious girl, who had started off as an office assistant in a small software company. As the company grew, she grew with it, receiving increments and promotions. As a project leader, she successfully completed several assignments, and her dedication and sincerity were duly noted by her superiors.

One day, there was a massive systems failure in Meena's department. Though the service engineers were working on the problem, things could not be put right immediately and Meena lost her temper. She 'blew her top' as the saying goes, screaming and yelling at her juniors and colleagues.

Her boss, who happened to drop in, heard her and saw what was happening. She did not see him, for he slipped away unnoticed.

What Meena did not know was that the boss had recommended her for yet another promotion, this time as the officer in overall charge of the branch. But he was disturbed and disappointed with her behaviour that day. He thought to himself that such a responsibility could not be entrusted to someone who could lose her temper so easily.

Every year in July-August, flights from Mumbai airport are delayed or cancelled due to heavy monsoon rains. Every year, in December-January, the fog affects flights from Delhi airport. Hundreds of passengers queue up at the terminals, impatient with the delays and lack of adequate information. Sometimes, some of them lose their temper, abusing or even assaulting airline personnel.

Mind you, when there has been an air crash or a hijack or similar crisis, people tend to behave far more soberly and with great self-control. But a delay in departure or a flight cancellation makes them fly off the handle!

One of my friends, who is a doctor, told me the other day that many of his patients come to him with sudden outbreaks of high blood pressure. Outwardly they are calm, quiet, dignified individuals. But inwardly, the daily frustrations and irritations of life are taking their toll on these men.

I'm afraid all kinds of irritations are inevitable in our daily lives. You have an important appointment to keep and you are stuck in a traffic jam. You go to the hospital for a routine check-up and you are kept waiting for hours on end. You are trying to fall asleep, and the neighbour's children are playing loud, blaring music. You are trying to finish your household chores and leave for work, and there is a sales representative at the door trying to sell you a sewing machine or an encyclopaedia.

Let us accept that irritations are inevitable in our daily lives. We will have to face them, tackle them and master them, before we get on with the daily business of life.

Raj and Reena are a wonderful couple. Reena is quick, agile and literally flies about her daily tasks. Raj is slow, quiet, and acts after due consideration and reflection.

Reena is always trying to whip up delicious, unusual meals in her tiny kitchen. She actually sings and dances little steps as she puts together her creative concoctions for the family. But with all the flitting and dancing, little accidents happen. Milk spills over, a glass jar falls down and breaks into pieces. The pressure cooker misbehaves all of a sudden, and there is spinach all across the ceiling...

Cheerful, chirpy Reena then loses her cool utterly. She covers her eyes and screams, 'Raj, Raj, please come here! There's a disaster in the kitchen!'

Calm and unruffled, Raj arrives on the scene and escorts his loving wife out of the kitchen. He makes her sit down on a comfortable armchair, switches on the fan and puts on the TV for her. He then goes to work in the kitchen with a broom, dustpan and mop. In ten minutes, the kitchen is cleaned up and shining like new. Raj, who is a senior executive in a multinational company, is also an ace hand at cleaning up in the kitchen after his wife's 'disasters'.

Reena steps gingerly into the kitchen and surveys the scene anxiously. Heartened by the clean-up operation, she flutters her eyelids at her loving husband and cries, 'Oh Raj, you're just wonderful!'

Irritations are inevitable. We are going to encounter them wherever we are, whatever we do. If we are wise and mature, we will learn to handle them without paying a heavy price in terms of frayed nerves and acute emotions.

Mr Das Gupta is an industrialist. His neighbour, Mr Joshi, is a chartered accountant. The men respect each other and greet each other cordially whenever they meet, and exchange pleasantries. You would describe them as decent, civilised citizens.

One day, Mr Joshi is playing cricket with his sons, and the ball lands on Mr Das Gupta's Honda car. Mr Das Gupta is indeed a man of many virtues. But putting up with bumps on his car is not one of them. Angrily, he confronts Mr Joshi and orders him to stop his silly game at once.

Mr Joshi lacks the grace to apologise. He insists that children must be allowed to play and points out that rubber balls can't do much damage anyway. Tempers rise, people arrive to take sides and the children flee from the scene in fear.

Imagine how the situation would have turned out if Mr Das Gupta had said to the budding Tendulkar next door, 'Well done, Sachin! But do keep your cover drives away from uncle's car!'

Sheila and Sita are colleagues in a government office. Sheila is late for work one morning, and Sita remarks sarcastically about some people who observe their own IST—Indian *Stretchable* Time. Sheila is livid, and quietly nurses the irritation within her mind all day. When she goes back home, she scolds her children, snaps at her husband and goes to bed complaining of a headache.

When we train our mind constantly on irritations, we only allow them to linger on and become festering annoyances. The trick is to snap out of irritations and recover our calm and serenity. Better still, we should learn to block out irritations altogether, by adopting a tolerant, easy-going attitude towards people and events.

Rahim was the assistant manager of the front office of a hotel. A lady had checked into one of the deluxe rooms. She was out all day, leaving at nine in the morning and returning only at eight in the night. She met Rahim once in the morning, when she handed over her keys, and once at night, when she collected them from the front desk. Each time, she would shoot off a list of complaints and demands, she would fuss over the messages left for her, and in general made life tough for him.

Rahim had been trained at an eminent institute and had a diploma in Hotel Management. But he had to grit his teeth and put up with the lady, who was beginning to get on his nerves. He spoke to his mother about her one night when he went home.

'Be patient with her, son, and send out a prayer for her when she annoys you,' advised his mother, who was a wise and compassionate woman. 'God knows what's bothering her, poor soul!'

Rahim decided to follow his mother's advice. For the next few days, he listened patiently to the lady, attended to her complaints promptly, and arranged all that she wanted.

A week later, she came down to settle her bill. 'Please order a taxi to take me to the airport,' she requested.

'I hope you found your stay pleasant and comfortable, Ma'am,' Rahim said to her. 'We do hope you will come back to stay with us whenever you are in this city.'

To his shock, the lady burst into tears. 'Oh, I hope I'll never, ever come back here,' she said with a sob. 'My former husband, who deserted me years ago to run away with another woman, was in the hospital, dying of cancer. He asked to see me and I had to come here so that I could bury the bitter past and help him die in peace. But it has been too much for me! He is dead now, and I must go back and allow my own wound to heal!'

Rahim was startled to realise that while he had been battling with the petty irritation caused by her behaviour, she had been passing through a terrible emotional ordeal.

Once you refuse to give in to irritation and annoyance, you will find that the world is a different place altogether.

All it requires is patience, tolerance, understanding and faith. Learn to have an objective, detached and dispassionate attitude to problems. Try to understand why some people behave as they do and you will find that their behaviour no longer upsets you. Instead, you will find yourself sympathising with them and trying to help them in any way you could!

By giving in to irritation, we allow our energy levels to drain, our efficiency lowers drastically, and we also lay ourselves open to worse problems that are sure to follow.

Have you seen the comic strip where an irate driver kicks the flat tyre of his car, and then howls in pain as his foot is sprained by the kick?

Granted, it is a human tendency to want to hit back at whatever, or whoever, has annoyed you. But it can be an even more satisfying experience when you control your resentment and become the master, not only of yourself but of the situation. And remember, the man who can master a situation by exercising self-control always wins the battles of life!

Friends, every one of us knows what it is to feel irritated and unhappy. We are, after all, ordinary people and even great men have given in to irritation at one time or another. Therefore, we have to work hard at conquering irritations.

A mature, wise, tolerant and spiritual person learns to face the daily irritations of life without being upset.

We easily feel upset, irritated, annoyed, unhappy. The driver is delayed in reporting for work, and his employer is driven into a frenzy. Frenzy is fine, if it is going to bring the driver to his door at once. But he knows it cannot, so who is the loser?

Jimmy Durante, the comedian, schooled himself never to be upset, never to feel irritated. Whenever he was faced with a trying situation, he would exclaim, 'That's the situation that prevails, so what can you do about it?'

A distinguished writer received a visitor at his house. The visitor wanted to look at the room where all his wonderful novels were written. The writer led him to his study. The visitor was shocked to find the room exposed to a veritable din of noise—noise from the traffic outside, a TV blaring from the flat next door, pots and pans banging about in the kitchen and so on.

'How can you work in here?' the visitor gasped in astonishment. 'How can you concentrate amidst all this noise?'

The writer smiled. 'The noise does not bother me,' he said. 'I cannot stop the traffic outside. I cannot dictate terms to my neighbours. We all have to eat, and the servant must do her work in the kitchen. When I want silence, I shut the doors and windows and turn on the fan. I know it's a one-way adjustment, but it works well for me!'

Patience is the formula which can help you shut out and cope with every kind of irritation!

Malik Dinar was a Sufi saint. His neighbour was a Jew, who wished to annoy the saint constantly. He built his toilets just outside the entrance to Malik Dinar's house, so that whenever the saint left his home or came back, he had to cross a row of stinking toilets that were deliberately left unclean for days together.

The saint did not feel irritated or upset. Whenever he left his house or came back, he held his handkerchief across his nose and moved away quietly. He never ever forgot to greet the Jew and bless him whenever they met.

'Don't you feel annoyed when you have to pass by my toilets every day?' the Jew asked him one day.

'Upset?' asked Malik Dinar. 'What right have I to feel upset? I only have to cover my nose with a handkerchief and that doesn't take much!'

That was one-way adjustment too! When we learn this art of adjustment, we can turn every tragedy into a triumph. For, as I said, if your mind is focussed on irritations, they will never leave you. Patience is the magic formula to conquer irritations.

How may we overcome irritations and annoyances? I would like to pass on to you nine practical suggestions.

As I always say, you need not practise all nine suggestions simultaneously. It is enough if you adopt one or two of them and try to bear witness to them in deeds of daily life. You will also find that a different tactic is required to tackle different kinds of situations. Take them up, one at a time and see how they may be put to work for your benefit!

PART II

How We Can Swallow Irritation

1

Be Aware that God is Always Watching Over You!

I am not alone, God is with me!

This, I believe, is the mantra for modern man, struggling with the problems of isolation, alienation and rootlessness that characterise life in the twenty-first century.

I am not alone, God is with me! This belief will help you face the problems of life with equanimity, calmness and quiet confidence.

On the upper galleries of the cathedral of Milan, there are many statues of saints carved in exquisite white marble. The dedicated sculptor who created these masterpieces was busy at his work when one of his friends came to see him.

'I don't see why you are wasting your artistic effort in such a place.

High up here, in these unseen galleries, nobody will ever get to look at your statues. Therefore, your work will not really be appreciated. Isn't that a pity?'

'It is enough for me that you recognise their value,' smiled the artist.

'And what if I had not climbed up all those stairs to see your work?' countered the friend.

'My friend,' said the artist, 'surely God and his angels would have seen it, and that is enough!'

A boy took a handful of cookies from a jar without permission. His mother saw him do it.

'Mahesh,' she said patiently. 'Don't you know that God saw you taking those cookies?'

'Yes, He probably did,' agreed the boy. 'But I'm sure He did not see me eat them for I ate them under the table!'

During the American Civil War, when things were getting tough for the Northern armies, Abraham Lincoln asked the people to pray for their victory.

One of his critics asked him sarcastically, 'Are you sure, Mr President, that God is on your side?'

'I'm much more concerned that we should be on God's side,' said Lincoln. 'That thought occupies me all the time!'

If you can believe that there is a higher power watching you, taking care of you, sending you strength and wisdom to face the tribulations, irritations and annoyances of daily life, you will find it easier to take on irritations, tackle them effectively and conquer annoyance.

If such faith does not come to you naturally, you can actually cultivate it by repeating to yourself, 'God is watching me! God is watching over me!' Repeat this if possible, every hour. Repeat this to yourself, when you have to confront an irritating situation.

People who take risks, people who are exposed to danger constantly, know what it is to have the strength of this belief: 'God is watching me; God is watching over me!'

Have you seen circus acrobats who perform daredevil tricks? Have you seen trapeze artists walking across the high wire, seeming as if they are suspended in space? They cannot afford to lose their nerve; they cannot afford to have their calmness and composure disturbed.

All acrobats will tell you that they climb up to the high trapeze and walk on the high wire with the simple belief that God watches over them. This is what helps them to stay calm and composed, for their survival depends upon it.

You and I may not be trapeze artists, but we too have to walk the tightrope in the circus that is life. And the circus acrobats teach us the simple but valuable lesson that we can keep our cool, maintain our sense of balance, preserve our equanimity if we hold firmly on to the belief: 'God is watching me; God is watching over me!'

Irritation and annoyance raise clouds of darkness in our mind. People who live in desert areas will tell you how irritating sandstorms can be. Strong gusts of wind blow sand and dust into people's eyes and nose and face, so that it becomes impossible to see ahead, or indeed move on. Irritation raises just such a sandstorm in the mind, making it impossible to think clearly, shutting us off from the ultimate source of confidence, calmness and peace that is God's presence.

Alas, today we live in a world that is a veritable concrete jungle, cut-off from the healing forces of nature. We live in the midst of steel, stone, pollution, noise, harmful emissions, dirt and confusion. But all we have to do to access inner peace and confidence is to remind ourselves again and again that He, who is the source of the peace that passeth, surpasseth understanding—He is watching over us.

Therefore, my advice to you is this: Every morning, start the day by saying, 'God is watching over me'. Repeat this whenever you can, throughout the day. And as you fall asleep at night, say it to yourself yet again: 'God is watching over me!'

When you begin the day in this beautiful awareness, you breathe out aspirations of purity, love, joy and peace. Just as light dispels darkness, frustrations and irritations will be driven away from you, clearing the dark clouds that threaten your horizon.

A steamer, sailing over the sea, was caught in a squall one night. The ship tossed violently, awakening the passengers from their peaceful slumber. Nervous and frightened, they wondered what was happening. Some of them began to scream in fear.

On board the steamer was the captain's daughter, a little girl of eight years. The noise awakened her, and she asked her mother, sleepily, 'Mamma, what's happening?'

The mother explained to her that a storm was lashing the ship.

'Is Papa at the helm?' asked the frightened child. 'Yes, Papa is at the helm,' replied the mother.

Hearing this, the little girl snuggled back into her bed, and was fast asleep in no time at all! The winds still blew and the waves still rolled and the ship still tossed, but she was calm and confident because she knew her father was at the helm.

The Heavenly Father is always at the helm, and though storms may blow and thunder may strike, we can leave everything in His hands, knowing that He is watching over us.

As we proceed on the pathways of life, we encounter different types of weather—stormy and smooth, mild and wild. The one lesson we need to learn is utter dependence on God—utter faith in His loving care. Everything else will follow.

God is the ever-compassionate one. If ever He sends us irritations, annoyances and troubles, He does it with a purpose; He does it for our good; He does it so that we may grow in wisdom, patience, tolerance and understanding. Whatever He 'takes away', whatever He chooses to 'give', always has our good in view. When this insight dawns upon us, when we gain the awareness that God is watching us, watching over us, and that He is in control of our lives and indeed, the life of the Universe, we will have but one aspiration in our hearts: *Not my will, but Thy will be done!*

When troubles come to us, when we are confronted by irritations, annoyances and unhappiness, we must accept them as gifts from God. Then, indeed, we will find that we are not alone, God is with us.

When Sri Krishna said to Kunti, 'Ask for a boon', she replied, 'Lord, send me some little suffering every day! In suffering art Thou remembered. In pleasure Thou art forgotten!'

We must keep on reminding ourselves that God is in charge of the Universe. He is the controller of the destinies of individuals and nations, therefore, nothing can go wrong. Today, here and now, you may feel things are going wrong but if you have faith that God is in control, He is in charge of your life, you will be assured that nothing can go wrong, for in everything that happens, there is a meaning of God's mercy.

There are so many bitter experiences, so many incidents that trouble us, and we are unable to understand the *why* behind them. We must learn to look upon all these experiences—pleasant and unpleasant—as opportunities to learn about ourselves and our lives. Experiences are not harsh or bitter in themselves; they come to us to teach valuable lessons that we must learn in order to evolve. Therefore, we should accept every experience that comes to us as *prasadam* out of the holy hands of God.

People often exclaim, 'I feel like tearing my hair!' or 'I feel like banging my head against a wall!' when they have to face irritations and frustrations. 'Let me not be mad, not mad, sweet Heaven!' King Lear exclaims when his daughters begin to get on his frayed nerves.

If we tear our hair, if we shed bitter tears, if we bang our heads against a wall, we are only adding to our problems. This is a very negative reaction and will not solve our problems at all. What is happening will surely happen, we cannot avoid it, we cannot escape it and we cannot alter it. But we do have a choice: Either to react to it in a negative way, or respond to it in a positive way. The latter will save much of your precious emotional energy.

I often narrate the story of an American furniture merchant, who started from scratch and built up a flourishing business. After years of hard work, he decided to treat himself to a brief holiday and went to a seaside resort for a fortnight. When he returned after a relaxing vacation, he found his prosperous business in shambles! A fire had gutted his shop, his house and all his stocks of furniture and everything was reduced to ashes.

That was not just a petty irritation or annoyance; it was a major disaster, a terrible misfortune. But the man who faced the terrible calamity was a man of faith. He stood on the ashes of his dreams and hopes and desires, and with upturned eyes, he asked softly, 'God, what would You have me to do next?'

The answer came to him quickly. He picked up a pole, fixed it in the ground and attached a piece of cardboard to it. On the cardboard he wrote the words:

Shop burnt. House burnt.

Furniture burnt. Goods burnt.

But faith—not burnt!

Shall restart tomorrow!

This was a man who refused to give in to irritation and annoyance!

Thomas Edison, too, lost millions of dollars worth of equipment, and the record of his life's work, when the Edison Industries were destroyed by fire in 1914.

Edison's son, Charles, spotted his father standing near the smouldering fire, his white hair blowing in the sharp winter wind. His heart ached in compassion for what his father had lost.

Edison saw Charles and waved to him. 'Where's your mother?' he called out. 'Find her at once. Bring her here. She will never see anything like this again, as long as she lives!'

The next morning, as he walked among the ashes of his hard work, his hopes and dreams, the sixty-seven-year-old inventor said, 'There is great value in disaster. All our mistakes are burned up. Thank God, we can start anew.'

George Washington Carver, the great scientist, lost all his life's savings when his bank crashed. He was poorer by 70,000 dollars. When he learnt of the loss, he remarked mildly, 'I guess somebody found a use for that money. I was not using it myself!'

A tiny mouse got into a grand piano and started to gnaw on the keys inside the instrument. Suddenly, the keys began to move, for a great artist had sat at the piano and had begun to play a *Chopin Solo*. In his pathetic little brain, the mouse was annoyed and irritated by what he perceived to be the disorder of the Universe.

Aren't we like the silly mouse when we judge God's plans from our point of view?

A lady on a long transcontinental flight was terrified when the jet hit strong turbulence. Nervously, she asked the flight stewardess, 'Are we going to crash?'

'Of course not,' the stewardess smiled. 'Don't worry. We are all safe in God's hands.'

The woman's eyes widened with shock 'Oh my!' she exclaimed, 'Is it that bad?'

'No!' said the stewardess emphatically. 'It's that good!'

As ordinary mortals, we have so many imperfections, defects, errors, weaknesses and insufficiencies. We are often overcome by doubts and insecurities. It becomes essential that we all learn to put ourselves in God's hands and allow ourselves to be guided by His divine wisdom.

It was a hot day. Nasruddin Hodja sat under a walnut tree, looking at his pumpkin vines.

He said to himself: 'God is indeed foolish! Here, He puts the heavy, large pumpkin on this delicate creeper which can only lie on the ground. And He puts these tiny walnuts on a big tree whose branches can easily hold the weight of a man! Now, if I were God, I'm sure I could do better than that.'

Just then a gust of wind blew; it dislodged a walnut which fell on the head of Hodja.

'Ouch!' exclaimed Hodja, rubbing his head, a sadder and wiser man. 'God is right after all! Now, if it had been a pumpkin up there, instead of a tiny walnut, what would have become of me! Never again will I try to plan the world for God, but I shall thank God that He has planned the world so well!'

In God's providence, everything comes to pass at the right time. The sun rises at the right time; the stars appear at the right time; the seasons change at the right time.

Put forth the best that you are capable of. Leave the results in the safe hands of the Lord. He will never fail you!

Leave it to God and He will take care of everything.

Remember there is no problem which cannot be solved.

In God is the solution to all problems.

Forget the problem, fix your attention on God. Your difficulties will disappear.

Do not fear, nor be awed by circumstances. And never forget that the battle is not yours but God's!

Many people tell me: We work so hard, so strenuously and yet, we achieve nothing. We work for the good of the community, society, nation and humanity. We sacrifice our health, wealth, rest and leisure. Yet our work produces no effect, it gives us no satisfaction. The world speeds on, from danger to destruction, and our life is reduced to a never-ending cycle of work, tension and frustration.

The reason for this is that our work is not in tune with the divine will. Our work is tainted with our preoccupation with our self—desire for prominence, desire for recognition, or even thoughts of reward in the life beyond. We have not relinquished control to God!

The man who offers his life, his all at the Lotus Feet of the Lord, works with peace in his heart. He works as a servant of God and man. His work does not take him away from God; his work is God-guided. In his work, there is no hustle or bustle, no fuss, no noise, no aimless rushing about. In his work there is no unrest, nothing but peace that passeth understanding!

2

Always Be Relaxed in Body and Mind

Most of us give in to irritation so easily because we are constantly in tension; we have forgotten how to relax.

In the words of a famous poet: 'The world is too much with us'. We are filled with the stress and strain of constant striving and struggling. We must learn to pause, so that we may renew ourselves.

Have you noticed how some people maintain their calmness, their equanimity amidst the hustle and bustle of life? Such people seem to possess an inner tranquillity, a peaceful centre in their souls that is unaffected by the turbulence outside.

I am told that the ancient Chinese language comprised of characters or symbols for words. Each 'symbol' represents an idea and combination of symbols form words. In ancient Chinese, the word 'busy' was represented by two characters—'killing' and 'heart'.

I find that truly significant, indeed, a dire warning to us all. I'm afraid we are trapping ourselves in an endless list of tasks, errands, appointments and things to do. In the process, we are stressed, hassled, annoyed and irritated. We have forgotten how to relax!

A sister once told me, 'I always awaken with a start every morning. I nearly jump out of my skin when I awaken, and think of all that I have to do that day.'

I find that sad indeed. If we are unable to start the day with God, in a spirit of faith and optimism, then we are too busy for our own good. As a Buddhist teaching tells us: Whatever the situation, we cannot make peace, unless we ourselves are at peace.

Grenville Kleiser said: 'Do not let trifles disturb your tranquility of mind. Life is too precious to be sacrificed for the non-essential and transient... ignore the inconsequential.'

We cannot always have everything happening as we wish, but we can surely accept everything that happens to us in a spirit of peace and contentment and our life will be truly serene.

Dr Arthur Caliandro was a preacher at the Marble Collegiate Church, New York. He wrote about the 'power of the quiet centre' that all of us need to cultivate. His easy and helpful suggestion to achieve this is simply to pause, to take a breath. 'Pause within the day', he tells us. 'Pause within the hour. Pause within the problem. Back off from whatever bothers you for a while. Sigh and get a breath of relief.'

We are basically made in such a way that we need to take a pause every now and then. This is why we sleep during the night. Sleep is nothing but the body's way of pausing to rest. We all know how refreshed and relaxed we feel after a good night's rest. We are ready to take on the new day and all its responsibilities. The vital pause in the middle of a rushed day can do the same for you!

The pause, the breath of relaxation recharges your batteries and enhances your vitality. Albert Einstein once wondered aloud, why he got his best ideas in the morning, while he was shaving. The answer was simple: The mind needs to be free, to wander, to dream. When it is thus freed, the most creative ideas emerge.

Many great writers and novelists often hit a bad patch, an empty feeling often called 'writer's block' beyond which they can't seem to continue. No matter how hard they try to think, concentrate and get on with their work, they fail to make any progress. They waste a lot of emotional and physical effort, but all to no avail. Then they put their papers away and take a break—go for a walk maybe, or play with a pet dog, or just go out into the garden to gaze at the sky. When the bad patch, the 'problem' has been completely put off from their mind, they find that new creative ideas begin to flow.

This is the dynamics of the creative process that Rollo May told us about in his book, *The Courage to Create.* By all means give yourself to your work wholly, concentrate on it, give it your best and then, pause, pull back, allow yourself to relax. Forget all about it and the pause will begin to work for you.

Arjun and Seema are both creative artists. Like many artists, both of them are hypersensitive and temperamental. Very often, they get into heated arguments and reach 'a point of explosion' as Arjun calls it.

But the couple has found a way to tackle the problem of unresolved conflicts. They break off abruptly and both individually seek their favourite corner to pause or reflect. They concentrate on God, on peace and joy and optimism. And they find that peace descends on them and that they are able to relax completely.

A few minutes later, they are ready to face each other again, and discuss the problem calmly, quietly and meaningfully. This is how the relaxing pause helps and heals strained relationships.

People today are given to what is called 'overwork'. They work too hard, they strain themselves excessively, only to find that they become stressed and irritated.

Do your duty by all means but do not stretch yourself beyond limits. Go about your work quietly, gently; speak to others sweetly, lovingly; take things easy.

There was a man whom I met in the days of my youth. He was not rich in the wealth of the world, but he was peaceful and contented. There was a spring in his step as he walked. His face shone with joy. And I never heard an angry word leave his lips.

One day I asked him, 'Tell me Sir, what is the secret of your life?'

He laughed. 'My secret?' he said, 'My secret is a simple one. I take everything easy…absolutely everything!'

Take it easy, my brother. Take it easy, my sister. Take it easy but don't be lazy!

A young man was once sitting under a tree when a middle-aged man happened to pass by. Looking at him, the middle-aged man thought to himself, 'This man is so lazy. He is just wasting his time!'

Aloud, he said, 'Tom, what are you doing here?'

'I'm enjoying life,' smiled Tom.

'Why don't you get up and do some work?' said the middle-aged man sternly.

'What for?'

'If you work, you will earn money.'

'What for?' asked Tom again.

'If you earn money, you will be able to save for the future.'

'What for?'

'You will be able to take a vacation.'

'What for?'

'If you go on a vacation, you can enjoy life!'

'But that's just what I am doing now!' laughed the young man. 'Why should I struggle hard to reach the place where I already am!'

I do not advocate laziness, but it is important that we all learn to relax, to practise what the Quakers call 'centring down', that is, cultivating inner silence.

Henry David Thoreau said, 'To affect the quality of the day that is the highest of the arts.' Learning how to pause, learning how to relax, can indeed affect the quality of your day!

When we have mastered the art of inner silence, we bring peace wherever we go. So it is that we have the Tao saying:

She who is centred in the Tao
Can go where she wishes, without danger.
She perceives the universal harmony,
Even amid great pain
Because she has found peace in her heart.

A Christian missionary in Africa had hired a group of natives to carry all the things he needed to set up a new mission campus. The trail lay along the hot and dusty plain, and the line of carriers was moving smoothly. Suddenly, the men put aside their burden and sat down by the wayside. No coaxing, cajoling or threats would make them budge.

'Why are you doing this?' asked the Padre, bewildered by their conduct. 'What's come over you all of a sudden?'

One man came up with the answer: 'We've been working at such speed to please you. Now we have to wait for our souls to catch up with our bodies.'

How true this is of very many of us! We are always on the move, 'on the go', so much so that we don't give our souls a chance to catch up with our bodies!

Once, when Mumbai was flooded by unprecedented rains, a young mother and her two small children were trapped in their third floor apartment. The children's father had been unable to leave his office for two days. There was no electricity in the building. Water had risen up to the first floor and no one could enter or leave the building.

At first, the young woman and her children panicked and grew nervous. Nervousness yielded to frustration and soon tempers snapped. The children were crying peevishly and the mother was scolding them.

Suddenly, something caught their attention. Outside their window, in the green and leafy branches of a huge tree, a mother bird and two fledglings were eagerly chirping in their nest. Despite the pouring rain and the inclement weather, the mother bird had managed to go out and get a few tasty titbits for her young ones. She was now feeding them as they chirped and squeaked eagerly, clamouring for their share. When the babies had been fed, mother and baby-birds nestled quietly and contentedly in their frail nest, while all around them, the skies opened up in a deluge. They had managed to create their own centre of peace and calm amidst the storm, and they rested securely in their centre of serenity.

Now the mother and her children—the human ones—derived a wonderful sense of comfort and consolation from this miraculous sight of nature.

Nature can teach us the valuable lesson of calmness!

In all situations of life, keep calm. The inner balance is essential to spiritual progress. Living in harmony with your 'self' is more important than brave deeds and actions.

If, in the midst of your daily work, your mind is agitated even for a brief while, stop immediately! Withdraw into silence and try to regain your inner calm. It is your richest treasure.

May I give you the secret of true relaxation? It is contained in these three words: *Let it go!* Life is full of incidents—pleasant and unpleasant. When unpleasant things happen, when irritations and frustrations mount, we are apt to lose our balance. This brings about negative emotions which create depression and unhappiness. An effective way of dealing with such a situation is to go to the root of the matter and 'let go' what is causing the negative emotion. Just let it go, let everything go!

Has my sister failed to understand me? Let it go! Has my brother spoken ill of me? Let it go! Has my best friend turned against me? Let it go! Have I been treated with disrespect? Let it go!

There was a wealthy man who was always full of anxiety, worry and care. Though he had everything that the world could give, he was not at peace with himself. He had a wise servant who knew the secret of peace—to trust in the Lord. One day, when he found his master fretting and fuming over a minor irritation, he said to the rich man, 'Master, can I ask you something?'

'What is it you wish to ask?' snapped the man.

'Is it not true that the Lord ran this world before you were born into it?'

'Yes, of course,' said the master.

'Is it not true,' continued the servant, 'that the Lord will run this world after you leave it?'

Again the master said, 'Yes!'

'In that case,' said the servant, 'why don't you let God run the world while you are *in* it?'

Here are some beautiful lines by Grenville Kleiser that can calm us:

Does the path seem rough and steep?
Leave it to God!
Do you sow, but fail to reap?
Leave it to God!
Yield to Him your human will,
Listen humbly and be still,
Love divine your mind can fill,
Leave it to God!

True relaxation is resting—resting in God until God's shakti flows into us, fills our entire being. So, it is necessary to enter the deep waters of the silence within, from time to time. 'The very first word in the scripture of life', Sadhu Vaswani said, 'is silence!'

The true strength of life is the strength of stillness. The world worships the strength of action, but much of the world's action is cruel, aggressive and tainted with selfishness. Therefore, we must seek our true strength by resting in God!

The man who has learnt to rest in God becomes the very picture of peace. He radiates peace to a world wandering in noise and discord, hate, strife, tension and irritation. Out of him flows healing vibrations of peace as a calm river flowing through the desert of life. He blesses all who come to him, and he is himself blessed.

3

Do Not Neglect Your Daily Appointment with God

It's a maddeningly hectic life that we all lead! We all have our duties to attend to. We have several obligations to fulfil. We cannot retire to the *tapobana* or the forest of meditation as the holy men did in the dim, distant past. We have to live in this world; we have to carry out our worldly duties. But while we attend to our duties sincerely, faithfully, honestly, earnestly, let us also carry the consciousness of God within our minds all the time.

'Seek ye first the kingdom of God', the Bible tells us, 'and all these things shall be added unto you.'

A holy man was invited to visit the estate of a wealthy landowner. As evening approached, the rich man took the visitor to the spacious terrace atop his mansion and pointed in each direction.

'Do you see those orchards to the east? I grow apples, pears, plums and peaches there. As far as the eyes can see, the orchards are mine!

'Do you see the farmland that stretches to your west? I grow potatoes, cauliflowers and cabbage in those fields. Fifty per cent of the state's supply comes from my lands!

'Do you see those beautiful gardens to the south? I am growing exquisite flowers for export out there. There are dahlias, chrysanthemums, roses and lilies. My gardens stretch for miles in that direction.

'Do you see those virgin forests to the north? They belong to me, too! There are millions worth of the country's best timber out there—teak, rosewood, oak and pine, they are all mine!

'I have worked hard over the last thirty years and built up this green treasure, and it is mine, on merit!'

He waved his hands all over, turning triumphantly in all directions. 'It's mine, and I own all that you see in any direction from my home!'

He paused, searching the holy man's face for some reaction, expecting words of praise, admiration and appreciation.

The holy man laid his hand upon the wealthy landowner's shoulder and pointed upward. 'Tell me Brother,' he said gently, 'how much do you own in that direction?'

We are told that on an average, over 3,00,000 people die every day—men, women and children. Does it not make you wonder, when my turn will come, when your turn will come? We all know that we have arrived here on this earth with a return ticket. Back to our true homeland, we must all return sooner or later. Therefore, I say, let the thought of God be in your consciousness all the time!

Never neglect your daily appointment with God! Preferably at the same time and the same place every day, go to your silent corner and commune with God.

God is the nearest of the near. He is the dearest of the dear. He is closer to us than breathing, nearer than hands and feet. God is not a far-off, shadowy being, dwelling on a distant star. He is within every heart. Each one has God, his own special God dwelling within him.

It is not at all difficult to commune with God. You and God are, in fact, interconnected. The tiniest whisper of the human heart is audible to His ears. You do not need a telephone to speak to Him. He has a dedicated hot line that is always open to you. You barely give your message and it has reached Him already! And God gives us the answer immediately. All we need to do is be receptive to Him!

All the time while we are attending to our daily work, let our hearts be fixed upon God. A ship on the stormy sea moves hither and thither, tossed by the waves. But the needle of the ship's compass is ever turned northward. Even so, let the ship of the body move hither and thither, and attend to its multifarious duties, but let the needle of the heart's compass be ever directed towards God. This will happen through practice.

Further, as eminent thinkers have pointed to us, there is no need for us to beg and plead the Lord to love us and commune with us. Out of His infinite love and grace, He is always ready and willing to enter into our lives. As Amy Carmichael said: 'His love is pressing around us on all sides like air. Cease to resist, and instantly His love will take possession of you!'

All of us will agree that even when we are trying to say our prayers, our mind often wanders to worldly matters. Therefore, I say to you even while you are engaged in your worldly tasks, let God-consciousness be at the back of your mind!

A television reporter was interviewing six-year-olds in a primary school.

'Do you know where God is?' he asked a little boy.

‘Do you know where He isn’t?’ the youngster shot back.

True, God is Omnipresent, Omnipotent, Omniscient. Nevertheless, it is a good habit to seek your daily appointment with Him, preferably at the same time, preferably at the same place, every day.

Sitting in your chosen silent corner, you can repeat the Name Divine, you can pray, you can meditate, you can engage yourself in a loving and intimate conversation with God, you can do your spiritual thinking. But this practice of daily silence is very essential to maintain your inner balance. If you wish to overcome irritations, if you don’t wish to be annoyed, if you wish to be truly happy, you must never miss out on this practice which I call our daily appointment with God. We take great trouble to keep a number of appointments every day, but we miss out the most important of all appointments—our daily appointment with God.

Silence has been described by a great Sufi thinker as ‘the garden of meditation’. The human mind constantly wavers. It keeps on drifting from one thought to another. Restlessness becomes its characteristic feature, and therefore, it has been said, ‘The mind is a monkey’.

How can we focus the mind on God? How can we learn to concentrate on His loving presence? This question is raised by Arjuna in the Bhagavad Gita. ‘The mind is more restless than a storm’, Arjuna tells Sri Krishna. ‘Will I ever be able to control it?’

Sri Krishna assures him that it may not be easy, but it is indeed possible. ‘You can control the mind by these two means’, says the Lord, ‘by *abhyasa* and *vairagya*’.

Abhyasa is nothing but practice. It is doing the same thing over and over again. We are all slaves to our habits, which have become part of our nature. But we must try to form, reform new habits and one of the best new habits you can cultivate is this wonderful practice of keeping up your daily appointment with the Lord.

Our mind, as I said, has acquired this habit of wandering, not through this birth merely, but through birth after birth.

Let me tell you the story of Mullah Nasruddin. He would sit every day for eight hours, in silence, with his ear against the wall. He did this day after day.

One day his wife asked him, 'Mullah, you sit with your ear stuck to the wall every day. Tell me, what do you hear?'

The Mullah replied, 'If you wish to hear what I hear, you must come and sit here yourself.'

Intrigued, his wife awoke very early the next morning. She finished all the day's household chores, so that she would be free to go and sit all day with her ear against the wall. She was determined to hear whatever it was that Mullah heard.

She sat for four long hours but she heard nothing!

Exasperated, she said to the Mullah, 'I have sat here for four hours and I have heard nothing! I am tired and I'm giving up now!'

The Mullah retorted, 'You want to give up after four hours. I have been sitting in that position for eight hours every day for the last twenty-eight years. I have not heard anything either, but I do not give up so easily!'

That is quite an amusing story but I do admire Mullah's spirit of persistence. It is this persistence that you need when you decide to seek the Lord in silence for a few minutes daily.

Many people are apt to imagine that the practice of silence and daily meditation are meant only for ascetics and hermits, who have nothing to do with worldly pleasures. I would like to tell you that this is not so. We, who are of the world, need it more than hermits do. Quiet contemplation and reflective silence are invaluable to us as a means to achieving peace of mind. Meditation is now being regarded by scientists as a great healing practice, the therapy of the twenty-first century.

Their research has shown that meditation alters the activity of the nervous system in such a way that the creative energy of the individual is recharged.

For our purpose, success in meditation is closely related to peaceful living. Through this practice, we not only keep our daily appointment with God, but also contact through Him a source of tremendous power which is within each one of us, but of which many of us are not aware!

People often ask me, 'Which is the best time to keep our daily appointment with God? And which is the best place for that purpose?'

My answer to them is: There can be no better time for prayer than now and no better place than wherever we happen to be. But I must also add that it is commonly supposed that the best time for communication with God is either the silent hour of the dawn, or the sacred hour of the evening twilight, and the best place is your own favourite silent corner.

All of us tumble and fall, at one time or another, in the endless race that is life. We must go to God, as we go to our mother, for healing and comfort.

If a child falls into a ditch and is covered with mud and filth, what does he do? He runs to his mother and says, 'Ma, I have become dirty, cleanse me!'

We must be like that child. We don't have to wait and ponder, we don't have to think twice, we don't have to be afraid to approach our Mother!

To Maharshi Ramana, there came a seeker who said, 'I desire to live in solitude and devote all my time to meditation and contemplation of God.'

The Maharshi told him, 'What does it matter where and how you are placed? The essential point is that the mind must always remain in its source. There is nothing external which is not internal. The mind is all.

If the mind is active, even solitude becomes like a market place. There is no use closing your eyes. Close the mental eye and all will be right.'

There was once a man of God who brought joy, hope and comfort into the lives of many. Whomsoever he met, he changed their lives for the better.

'How do you do it?' they asked him. 'What is the secret of the radiance, the serenity and the spirit of joy that seems to emanate from you wherever you go?'

In answer, the holy man narrated this incident from his life. He was leaving his home as a young man, to tread the spiritual path. His old mother walked along with him to the outskirts of the town, where she had to part from him. It was time to let go of her son, time to say goodbye, perhaps forever!

'Promise me one thing before you leave,' she said, holding onto his hands.

'What is it, Mother?' he asked her gently. 'Promise me first,' she insisted.

'Dear Mother, you must tell me what it is that you want me to do, before I make my promise,' the young man said.

'Oh, it's nothing difficult,' the mother pleaded. 'Promise me first!'

'As you wish, dear Mother,' said the young man, relenting. 'I promise to do as you wish!'

The mother kissed her son. 'My child,' she said to him earnestly. 'It is a tough and demanding world out there, a wicked world some would say, into which you go to seek your salvation. Promise me this: Begin every day with God. And close every day with God. This is all I ask of you.'

'My mother taught me the secret of true joy and lasting peace,' the holy man concluded. 'I begin the day with God and close the day with God.'

4

Always See the Bright Side of Things

The irritations, annoyances, stress and strain of modern life seem to have caught people in a bind. Many of my friends ask me to give them a simple formula that can ease the strain and tension of their minds.

The formula I offer to them is simple. Always have a positive attitude towards life, look at the bright side of things!

When I talk about the positive attitude and the bright side of life, I do not mean that life is all bright and rosy. Life does have a negative side, a dark side. Life is full of difficulties and dangers, trials and tribulations. But the man, with the positive approach, refuses to dwell on the negative side of life. Even when he is surrounded by the most adverse conditions, he will look for a place of shelter. Conditions around him may be frustrating but he will not give up. He will continue to expect the best.

This is an inviolable law of life—expect the best and you will get it. What you expect persistently comes rushing to you. For you only draw to yourself that which you think of all the time. Your thoughts are magnets. Through your thoughts, you draw to yourself what you are thinking of all the time!

Therefore, let me urge you—always look at the bright side!

There is a picture I saw many years ago. It was a picture of two buckets, each half-filled with water. On one bucket was drawn a face with a frown and underneath the words read: 'Of what use is it to be half-empty all the time?'

On the other bucket was drawn a face with a smile. The words below read: 'I feel grateful to God that I am at least half-full all the time!'

The two buckets symbolise the negative and positive attitudes to life. The man with the negative attitude refuses to look at the bright side. He is constantly frowning. He is always tensed, high-strung and prone to irritation. He feels dejected. He can never be really happy. He cannot face the stress and strain of life in the right spirit.

The man with the positive attitude always looks at the bright side of life. He is always smiling. He is buoyant and full of energy. He has the courage to face the demands and difficulties of life in the right spirit!

As a corollary to this, let me also urge you to see the good in others. As the Baha'i Prophet, Baha'u'llah has said, 'If a brother has nine virtues and one fault, let us think of his nine good qualities and forget the one fault. If a brother has nine faults and one virtue, let us consider his one virtue and forget the nine faults.'

That which we see in others, has a knack of shifting into us. If we consider the faults of others, they will inevitably become a part of our own nature.

Two men who served in the Second World War were severely injured. Each had to have an arm amputated. They were both sent to a rehabilitation centre for the disabled where they underwent training to use their one arm as efficiently as possible.

At the end of one year of training, one of them was so discouraged that he came to the conclusion that life was not worth living with such a handicap as he had.

The other soldier was so happy with the training he had received that he went about telling everyone, 'It is a boon that God has given people two arms when we can get along perfectly well with just one!'

That man was indeed an optimist!

I am told that in the first edition of Webster's dictionary, which was published early in the nineteenth century, the word *optimist* was to be found but not the word *pessimist*. We can only conclude that pessimism is a child of later growth!

Nothing contributes more to a stress-and-strain-free life than optimism, the habit of always looking at the bright side of things. 'The good side', we are told, 'is God's side.'

Albert Einstein had been the best man at a young friend's wedding. When he met the couple a few years later, they had brought their baby son to show him. The tiny tot was respectfully placed in the great scientist's arms. He took one look at the famous dishevelled head and promptly burst into a screaming fit.

His adoring parents were embarrassed and tried to hush the child. However, Einstein patted the boy on the head and crooned, 'You're the first person, in years, who has told me what you really think of me!'

There is a beautiful Swedish folk tale that tells us about a noisy discussion that took place among the creatures of a forest on a warm summer afternoon.

'Living is singing!' warbled a nightingale.

'What do you mean, singing?' grumbled a mole. 'Living is a constant struggle, burrowing in the darkness under the ground.'

'Absolutely not!' said the many-hued butterfly. 'Life is all joy and happiness and colour!'

'You're wrong,' said a diligent bee. 'Life is work.'

'That's true,' sighed an ant, 'Life is more work than joy'.

An eagle said from up above, 'Life is liberty, and soaring up in the blue sky!'

The plants now joined the discussion. The tall pine tree said the eagle was right. The wildflower felt the ant was right. As for the rose, it agreed with the butterfly.

Now a cloud spoke up. 'Life is just a shower of tears.'

The river gurgled as it went by, 'Life is just an unending stream.'

Just then, the church bells began to ring. Their peals said to the forest, 'True life is peace and joy, strength and happiness, courage and fidelity, and faith in God!'

Life is certainly determined by the way you look at it.

Thomas Alva Edison was an indefatigable inventor. He experimented constantly, trying out new solutions to old problems. At one stage in his career, he experimented ceaselessly to try and find a substitute for lead in the manufacture of storage batteries. He carried out over 20,000 experiments on this problem—all to no avail! Success eluded him, despite his phenomenal perseverance.

A reporter who came to interview him asked him, 'Aren't you discouraged by this failure? I mean 20,000 experiments and all of them in vain!'

Edison was not at all perturbed by this tactless question. 'In vain?' he exclaimed. 'That may be the way you look at it! As for me, I have discovered 20,000 things that cannot be a substitute for lead!'

The man who looks on the bright side of life is always learning from his failures and misfortunes. Optimism enables us to maintain our equanimity and poise, even when confronted with the worst provocations.

A holy man was going about town, collecting funds for the poor. He approached a gambler, who spat on him in contempt.

Taking out his handkerchief, he wiped his face and said to the gambler, 'Sir, that was for me, and I accept it with gratitude. What are you going to give me for the poor?'

The gambler was so moved that he donated a considerable sum of money to the holy man's good cause. What is more, he became the holy man's disciple for the rest of his life.

A pathologist ran a successful diagnostic centre where hundreds of patients flocked to have their medical tests done.

On a particularly busy day, the laboratory was flooded with patients suffering from a severe virus infection that was spreading all over the district.

The technicians and staff of the laboratory could barely cope with the rush. Tempers were raging and irritated staff was snapping at the patients.

The pathologist noted that one of his technicians was quietly bent over his work. Before him were as many as 200 phials of blood which he had to analyse that day. The young man was going about his work slowly, steadily, systematically.

The pathologist approached the young man and told him sympathetically, 'That's a lot of samples you have to analyse today! You must be feeling stressed!'

The young technician looked up and smiled at his boss. 'Sir, I handle only one sample at a time. I concentrate on the sample before me. I don't feel in the least stressed!'

The Reverend Whitefield was delivering a rousing sermon on optimism. He asserted emphatically, 'All that God made is perfect!' At this, a man with a hunchback rose from his pew and called out, 'What do you think of me?'

'Think of you?' said the indefatigable Whitefield. 'Why Sir, you have the most perfect hunchback my eyes ever beheld!'

When Donald B MacMillan, the Arctic explorer, was about to set out on one of his trips to the polar region, a letter arrived for him with the inscription: 'To be opened when everything has gone dead wrong'.

Nearly half a century passed, but MacMillan had no occasion to open the letter. He remarked to a friend, 'I did not want to break faith with whoever wrote it.' He added, 'And things just never got that bad!'

5

Count Your Blessings!

When you look on the bright side of things, you will keep on counting your blessings. And when you realise how truly blessed you are, you will not easily yield to irritation and annoyance.

A man once asked me if I had ever passed a sleepless night.

'Of course,' I said, 'I know what it is to toss and turn in bed, while sleep eludes me!'

'I'll tell you what to do,' he said enthusiastically. 'You must count sheep and you'll slip comfortably into sleep.'

I told him, 'I don't need to count sheep. I count my blessings instead. I count them up to a point where I don't need to number them anymore. Then I just relax and know that God will take care of everything!'

Robert Louis Stevenson, the famous author, was a chronic TB patient, suffering from the disease which wasted much of his later life. However, he would not allow the disease to get his spirits down.

One day, he was caught in a terrible bout of coughing. His wife who was in tears, said, 'Do you still believe it's a wonderful day?'

Stevenson was in the habit of saying, 'It's a wonderful day,' when the curtains of his window were drawn open each morning.

'Of course, it's a wonderful day,' said the writer, pointing to the window ablaze with sunlight. 'I will never let a row of medicines block my horizon!'

This was a man who knew how to count his blessings!

The distinguished Victorian writer, John Ruskin, was also a gifted painter. One of his nieces, a young girl, had received a beautiful silk handkerchief as a gift. But she accidentally dropped an inkpot over it, causing a big, ugly spot on the handkerchief.

She was inconsolable when Ruskin came in and saw what had happened. He took the handkerchief from her and retouched the inky spot so that it changed into a beautiful design. Now, the handkerchief was even more beautiful than before!

The girl was amazed to see the beautiful design and exclaimed, 'Is this really my handkerchief?'

'Yes, it is,' Ruskin assured her. 'I only changed the blot into a picture.'

It takes an optimist to see the picture behind the blot like the proverbial silver lining behind the grey clouds.

If we count our blessings, we realise that we are much better off than we thought we were! We draw fresh courage to fight the battle of life and find that our suffering recedes into the background.

The American Thanksgiving Day was drawing near. A class of first graders was told by their teacher to draw a picture of something for which they were thankful. Most of the children's drawings were predictable. Some drew a turkey, some drew a house or a car and some drew toys and bicycles. Only one little boy drew a hand.

The rest of the class tried to figure out whose hand it could be...God's? The policeman's? But no one could guess and the little boy refused to tell them.

When all the other children had left, the teacher came up to the little boy and asked gently, 'Whose hand is it, Tommy?'

The boy smiled and said to her, 'Yours, Miss Brown.'

Miss Brown's eyes were filled with tears. She recalled all the times she had used her hand to guide his pencil, help him get up from his chair or lead him across the road...for the little boy had disability affecting his hands.

Victor Riesel was a renowned newspaper columnist. His hard-hitting investigative report against certain criminal elements in New York City so angered the mobsters that they sent a hoodlum to hurl concentrated sulphuric acid into his eyes.

Riesel was blinded for life.

It was tough for him to cope with the terrible tragedy. But Riesel went back to work, writing his columns. He had a lot to be grateful for. Over 60,000 members of the public wrote to him to express their anguish. Over 1,000 people actually offered him one of their eyes.

'The torrent of generosity was a humbling experience for me,' Riesel wrote. The terrible accident taught Riesel a valuable truth: What happens to a man is not as important as how he meets it.

Through the constant pain and darkness, Riesel counted his little victories. This is how he puts it: 'Blind, I am less dazzled by material things. I have a deeper hunger for the blazing light that right and justice need. Even in the darkness, I can see that light!'

It was Wendell Phillips who said, 'What is defeat? Nothing but education, nothing but the first step to something better!'

People who count their blessings can even turn frustrations, annoyances and misfortunes into advantages.

6

Keep Yourself Busy Doing Something Creative

People often tell me that they 'feel bad'; sometimes they claim that they feel 'terrible'. Young people claim that they feel 'low'.

The reasons for the 'low mood' may vary from individual to individual:

- I do not have enough money
- I am too old
- No one understands me
- No one appreciates me
- I don't like my job

Psychologists tell us that circumstances are always neutral but our thinking and perception about them influence us a great deal.

We are all apt to imagine that it is our circumstances that frustrate us.

True, we often pass through phases of life when our circumstances are far from ideal. But then, our moods and feelings affect the way we look at circumstances. In a low mood, we see the dark side of everything. A housewife feels that she is trapped in her marriage and family; a working man thinks that his job is low and demeaning; a young student feels that he will never ever land a job that would suit his qualifications…

Our moods determine the way we react to circumstances. When we feel good, things are bright; when we feel low, frustrations haunt us.

Experts tell us that 'feeling good' is a practical and down-to-earth business. When we feel good, solving problems is easy and changing our circumstances is even easier.

Have you heard of the story of how Archimedes hit upon the theory of buoyancy? Legend tells us that he was lowering himself into a bathtub when the notion of the famous Archimedes Principle hit him in a flash, and the rest, as they say, is history.

When we feel good, we understand life better. People who seemed harsh and insensitive are merely seen to be funny. Does it not make sense then to try to feel good—as good as we can?

Think of what makes you feel good—it may be a hobby, it may be an activity you enjoy, something constructive or creative that you like to do. Devote your leisure time to such an activity or hobby and you will find that your whole attitude to life is transformed!

Colonel Thomas Hart Benton loved to devote himself to constructive activities of any kind. Once, when someone asked him how old he was, he replied, 'According to the calendar, my age is seventy-four. But when there is something good to be done, I am just thirty-five years old!'

When Pope John XXIII was the *Papal Nuncio* (ambassador) to France, he had invited some dignitaries to dinner. The deputy prime minister of the country was the first to arrive. On seeing his guest, the Nuncio exclaimed, 'Mon Dieu! I had forgotten!'

Borge sat down and began to crash out a
there was an impatient pounding on th
out, 'Stop that noise, you idiot! Don't y

When Nathaniel Hawthorne lost his g
dejected, on the brink of despair. His w
depression, did not attempt to talk hin
and ink on the table, lit a bright fire in
his shoulders and simply told him, 'Nov
book!'

Hawthorne took heart and what he prc
immortal classic, *The Scarlet Letter.*

However, the oversight was quickly rectified. He produced a couple of aprons and the distinguished Father and his early guest were soon busy preparing the meal!

There are many wealthy executives who enjoy working in the kitchen, experimenting with recipes, putting together delicious, unusual concoctions for their loved ones. They claim that the tension and stress of their high-powered business life is forgotten when they immerse themselves in their culinary experiments!

The late Indian President, Abdul Kalam, loved teaching. When he retired from his position as chairman of the Indian Space Research Organisation, he and his friend had planned to start a school for bright children from underprivileged background. However, the country could not do without him, and he was requested to become the scientific advisor to the Prime Minister. Even then, he continued to take up teaching assignments whenever he could spare the time! Dr Kalam was also a gifted poet and writer. He loved composing poems in English and his mother tongue, Tamil.

Not only do great men find something creative to do, they do everything creatively too!

Vera Henry won a special award for women writers. When a friend called to congratulate her, her young son Kevin said to the caller, 'The writer of the year is down in the basement doing the washing of the week.'

Bored housewives find their household chores dull and tedious. But successful women handle their chores with enthusiasm and efficiency.

Mrs Roosevelt brought a breezy informality and bustle of activities into the White House. At the inaugural buffet, it was she who served the President and his special guests!

She also startled the staff by insisting on operating the lift herself.

'That just isn't done, Mrs Roosevelt,' one of the staff members protested.

'It is now!' she said, as she slipped

When she was the First Lady at th
to ask for her secretary, Malvina T

'Miss Thompson isn't in,' said a v

'Who is that, please?' the reporte

'Mrs Roosevelt,' came the simple

An incident narrated about the e
retelling. He was once travelling
'horse car' as it was called in tho
Whitman happily took it from it
soothed it. In no time at all, the b
his chest and fell fast asleep! Tl
children.

There was once a well-to-do f
distinguished themselves as docto
One of them, however, was cau
stammer and they were worried t

How wrong they were proved! T
hobby, and he became the world-
books, thirty plays and scores of
At eighty-six, Somerset Maughan
'What has influenced my life mor
my stammer.'

A speech defect, a disability, led h
his life completely!

The famous novelist, Victor Borg
often tell his friends that a piano l
far as to say that he could actuall

The disbelieving friends stared at

7

Smile, Smile, All The While!

If you wish to overcome irritations and annoyances, you must smile, smile all the while!

Sometimes, when I look at the faces of the people whom I meet on the road of life, it seems to me that they are carrying the burdens of the world on their frail shoulders!

A woman came to meet me some years ago. She said, 'I have been married for just over a year and during this period, my husband has smiled at me only three times!'

I must say I was taken aback. I would earnestly appeal to all young husbands—and all young-at-heart husbands—to smile at their wives at least three times every hour!

Look at the faces of children. Their faces are perpetually wreathed in smiles. If you wish to enter the Kingdom of Heaven—the kingdom in which there are no irritations, annoyances and unhappiness—you must learn to be like children, too!

Seek to live as a child! The child knows that his mother is near and that it has nothing to fear. No mother would wish to bring her child to harm. And so the child knows that nothing can ever go wrong. All is well, all was well, and will ever be well, both tomorrow and a hundred years hence. The person who believes in this will always continue to smile the smile of bliss.

My beloved Master, Sadhu Vaswani, always had a radiant smile upon his lips. When they asked him the reason, he replied, 'I have a friend. He protects me. He guards me in illness. He blesses me every day. And He stretches forth His arms of love to enfold me in the silence and darkness of the night. He is your Friend, too! Indeed, He is the Friend of friends!'

Sadhu Vaswani's smile was the smile of one who felt the joy of God's presence all the time. It is a joy which is open to each one of us. Each one of us can and must become a smile-millionaire!

People often tell me, 'We have nothing to smile about.'

If we feel we cannot smile all the time, it is because we are afflicted with the disease of desire. Whenever our desires are fulfilled, we are ready to smile. When our desires are crossed, we feel miserable and unhappy. When we are in a neutral state—neither happy nor unhappy—we feel bored. It is only when we transcend these three states that we are filled with peace—the peace that passeth, surpasseth understanding.

When the heart of a man is filled with the love of God and love of the suffering children of God, his face wears a divine smile. Such a man carries the joy and peace of God wherever he goes.

Outer conditions—the hassles, worries, irritations and annoyances of daily life cannot affect such a smile. This is because the divine smile does not depend on outer conditions. It comes from within us. It is there within each one of us. We do not have to acquire it, we have but to regain it. We have lost it for the time being because we have identified ourselves with our bodies, our senses, with external conditions around us. We have come to believe that there can be no joy in life without sense-indulgence and sense-gratification.

Cheerfulness is indeed the new wonder drug. Doctors are of the view that people who smile stay healthy. Cheerfulness is the great lubricant of the wheels of life. It diminishes pain and disease, mitigates misfortune, lightens our burden and keeps us free from irritation and annoyance!

We are told that it takes forty-two muscles to frown and seventeen to smile. And the best thing about a smile is that it is contagious but let me urge you not to wait till you catch it from others. Be a 'carrier' yourself!

Here are some memorable thoughts I read long ago on the power of a smile:

> A smile costs nothing but gives much. It enriches those who receive without making poor those who give. It takes but a moment, but the memory of it sometimes lasts forever. None is so rich or mighty that he can get along without it and none is so poor that he cannot be made rich by it.
>
> A smile creates happiness in the home, fosters goodwill in business, and is the sign of friendship. It brings rest to the weary, cheer to the discouraged, sunshine to the sad, and it is nature's best antidote for trouble.
>
> Yet it cannot be bought, begged, borrowed or stolen, for it is something that is of no value to anyone unless it is given away from within.
>
> Some people are too tired to give you a smile. Give them one of yours, for none needs a smile so much as he who has none to give.
>
> —Frederick William Faber

Here are a few tips which would help you keep up the spirit of cheerfulness:

- Get up every morning with a smile on your face and the bright and cheerful greeting, 'Good Morning, God!' on your lips.
- See that your face always wears a smile. Rightly has Mahatma Gandhi said, 'You are not fully dressed until your face wears a smile.'
- Give a hearty laugh at least three times every day—once before breakfast, once before lunch and once before dinner. If you find it difficult to laugh, look into the mirror and make funny faces.
- Develop a healthy sense of humour. It will save you from many difficult situations.
- Learn to laugh at yourself.
- Always look at the bright side of things. Everything has two sides—the bright and the dark or as I would wish to put it, the bright and the less bright!
- Have faith that God is in charge of the Universe. He is the controller of the destiny of individuals and nations, so nothing can ever go wrong!

8

Practise the Technique of Tonglen

Many of my readers will find themselves asking: What is *tonglen*? Some of you may find this suggestion strange. A few will wonder: Will it really help? Let me assure all of you—if you really put this into practice, you will be amazed, you will be filled with wonder at the results you get! I also wish to tell you that I have practised it myself. This is why I recommend it to you in the fullest confidence that it can do wonders for you!

Tonglen is, in fact, a Buddhist practice recommended by one of the acharyas (senior teachers) of the *Shambhala* community. It works on a very simple but very profound idea: In order to feel compassion for others, we must learn to feel compassion for ourselves. In order to understand the pain and suffering of others, we have to connect ourselves to those who suffer. In order to overcome our fear of pain and suffering, we must learn to dissolve the 'tightness' of our heart and mind. In other words, *tonglen* releases the inner springs of compassion within us, breaking down the barriers of cruelty, indifference and coldness that we have built around ourselves.

Let us take the case of a friend, a near or dear one, who is suffering from illness, disease and pain. We wish to take on his suffering, we wish to help ease his pain. First, we breathe *in,* with the wish to take away his pain and misery. Then, as we breathe *out,* we send out happiness, joy, wholeness and peace or whatever we think will relieve that person.

This then, is the core of the practice:

- *Breathing in* others' pain so that they may heal and be well and experience freedom from unhappiness and anguish and stress.
- *Breathing out,* sending them positive feelings of joy and peace and well-being, which will bring them relief and happiness.

Tonglen is, thus, a simple two-step process: Breathing in, taking away, wiping out negative feelings and experiences; breathing out, spreading around us, sending out to others, peace, relaxation and spaciousness, a sense of comfort.

When you start practising this technique, you will at first find it difficult, for you will come face to face with your own annoyances, fears, irritations and frustrations. Your own anger and personal pain of the moment will offer resistance to this practice.

This is when you must use *tonglen* to help yourself, and millions of others like you, who are experiencing the same sense of anguish, misery, unhappiness and frustration. For, believe me, you are not the only one to fall prey to these negative feelings. Maybe you are unable to put a finger on the pain and say, 'This or that or the other is causing me this pain.' You are not even able to understand what is it that you feel—anger or hurt or pain, and what is it that you want—understanding, forgiveness or revenge.

At this point, breathe in for all the people who are caught, nay, stuck in the same anguish that you are feeling. Breathe in, for all of them who are experiencing those dreadful negative emotions. Then breathe out relief and understanding, peace and relaxation to all, including yourself. Breathe in your tightness, your tension, your irritation, and the tightness and tension of all the people around you. Breathe out spaciousness, comfort, healing and relief to all who need it.

Chances are that you may not even be able to name your feeling or identify what it is that irritates you. Just contact whatever you are feeling, whether it is tightness, anger, irritation or annoyance. Breathe it in and I would add, bite it, chew it and swallow it up!

Many people say that this is contrary to normal practice—of taking in what we want and need, and throwing out what we dislike. To a certain extent this is true. But the idea is to free ourselves from the habit of wanting everything the way we like, wanting everything to go according to our plans and ignoring the needs and interests of all others. This is the attitude that builds walls of selfishness and ego around us, cutting us off from the sense of kinship and brotherhood with the rest of humanity.

It also goes against the common human tendency to avoid pain and suffering in all forms, direct or indirect. By liberating ourselves from this selfish tendency, we liberate ourselves from the prison of the ego. We learn to accept ourselves and others; we learn to love ourselves and others; for, as I am never tired of saying, you are not apart from others; you are a part of others!

Tonglen awakens you to an awareness of this wonderful reality. It helps you to care for yourself and others. It offers you a much broader perspective on life and the world around you—a liberating perspective that enables you to become aware of your link with the world at large, your relation to the rest of humanity, your place in the vast universe. To use a Buddhist term, it allows you to experience the unlimited spaciousness of shunyata.

Tonglen can help people who are ill, people who are dying and people who are in sorrow. It can be practised as a systematic technique of meditation or it can even be done spontaneously, on the spot, at any time.

Let us say you are driving on the road, and you witness an accident victim being shifted to an ambulance. Some of you may actually wish to turn away from the sight or pretend that you have not seen it. This is because the sight awakens pain and fear within us; it causes confusion, for we know it may happen to us! On the spot at such a time, we can do *tonglen* for all the people, people like ourselves who wish to be compassionate, but are afraid; people who wish to be helpful, but are cowardly. Breathe in for all of us; breathe out for all of us. Breathe in for our pain and suffering, our failings and weaknesses. Breathe out for understanding and courage and compassion to come to all of us.

Simultaneously, breathe in, take in the pain and suffering of the accident victim, breathe out healing and relief for the accident victim and all who need it. Breathe in for all of us, breathe out for all of us. What seems like pain and poison is being used as medicine here. Our personal anguish and frustration help us to cultivate compassion for all beings!

Remember this wonderful technique when you are overcome with annoyance and irritation: Breathe in your annoyance and irritation and the annoyances and irritations of everyone around you. They may be your friends or your foes—breathe in their negative emotions, for you must live with them! And when you breathe out, send out compassion, understanding, relief and relaxation to everyone around you. Breathe out spaciousness and peace. Breathe in your annoyances and those of others; breathe out peace and joy for all! You will be amazed at the results, I assure you!

Tonglen can also be practised as a formal meditation technique in four stages:

- Relax completely. Rest your mind in a state of openness and stillness. Feel a sense of spaciousness and clarity.

- Work with textures, with feelings converted to something tangible. Breathe in all feelings that are hot, dark, heavy, uncomfortable, tight, restricting and claustrophobic. Breathe out feelings that are light, bright, cool, open, fresh and liberating.
- Breathe in—not just through your nostrils—but through all the pores of your body. Breathe out—not just the air from your lungs but radiate through all the pores of the body, with every fibre of your being.
- In the third stage, begin to work on a personal situation that is real to you. In traditional *tonglen*, you begin by breathing in for someone you wish to help. But you can also use it to help yourself, and help all others who are in the same predicament that you are. This is very important for you and others like you. If you are feeling insecure or inadequate, breathe in the insecurities and inadequacies of all others and send out calmness, self-confidence, security and adequacy to everyone, including yourself.
- Finally, extend the practice beyond yourself. Do *tonglen* not just for yourself, but for those whom you love, do *tonglen* not only for those whom you love, but extend it to everyone, all people who are in the same situation. Make it bigger than just you or the one person you love. Do it for your enemies; do it for those who hurt you or hurt others.

There are no limits to the range of *tonglen*. As you practise it, you will feel your horizons expand. You will no longer be trapped by petty, narrow egotism which triggers irritation, unhappiness and annoyance. You will grow in the spirit of compassion and understanding; you will find yourself caring for others instead of being constantly obsessed with yourself. Above all, you will evolve towards maturity and wisdom, peace and understanding to all around you.

9

Help Others!

My beloved Master, Sadhu Vaswani, told us again and again, 'If you wish to be happy, make others happy!'

The happiness that we derive from selfless service is the highest form of happiness. He, who is busy helping others, will not have time for petty irritations.

A cold wind was howling and rains beating down heavily when the telephone rang at the residence of a rural doctor.

The doctor struggled to wake up and saw the bedside clock. It was 12:30 am!

The doctor was a kind and compassionate soul. He picked up the phone and enquired as to who was calling.

'It's my wife!' cried the farmer who had called. 'She needs a doctor right away. Can you please come at once?'

'Sure, I'll come,' said the doctor. 'But can you come and get me? You see, my car is being repaired.'

'What?' sputtered the voice on the line, 'how do you expect me to come out on a night like this?'

The trouble with us is we always expect goods and services but we are unwilling to give them ourselves.

'Give, give, give! I am doing nothing but giving,' grumbled an irritated man. 'I am tired of giving.'

'All right, let's make a deal,' his guardian angel told him. 'You stop giving the moment God stops giving to you!'

We do not always have to give money; we can also give of ourselves.

A group of poor Mexican Indians were on their way to market to sell their crafts and pottery. They were met by a party of wealthy tourists who were captivated by the handicrafts and offered to buy the entire collection from them and that too, for a good price!

'Here, take these 500 dollars! And you will be saved the trouble of walking all the way to Nogales,' coaxed a wealthy American lady, the group leader.

'Forgive us, Senora,' said one of the Indians. 'We must go to Nogales.'

'But why?' asked the lady 'Why on earth must you go to Nogales when you can make a profitable sale here and now?'

The man explained to her, 'Senora, in my village no one can read or write. There is no electricity. There are no radios. Someone must go to Nogales to get us the news of the world. So we go to the market every Sunday. Without our pottery, we cannot get a place in the market. That's why we cannot sell you all our ware, for they are only the means to an end.'

He concluded apologetically, 'We would be disgraced if we would return home with nothing but money!'

People dislike the concept of 'morality' nowadays. 'What is moral and immoral?' they argue. 'It is all relative. Who is to say this is right and that is wrong? Morality is irrelevant today.'

I would beg to differ, in all humility. I believe there are two aspects of morality that are timeless and relevant: To be good and to do good.

'When you are good to others, you are best to yourself,' said a great thinker.

Zoroaster says the same thing: 'Doing good to others is not a duty. It is a joy for it increases your own health and happiness.'

Sadhu Vaswani taught us: Service of the poor is worship of God.

Truly, the way to attain God is not to perform empty rituals, say loud prayers or undertake pujas mechanically. God is with you for the asking when you extend a hand of loving service to the unfortunate ones.

A stranger was walking down the narrow winding streets of Varanasi, looking for a particular house.

'Excuse me,' he hailed a man who was just stepping out of his house. 'Would you be so kind as to tell me where Pandit Vidya Ratan lives?'

'Pandit Vidya Ratan? I have never heard of him,' said the man. 'Are you sure he lives here?'

'But I was told he was famous all over Varanasi,' the stranger insisted. 'He is one of the most learned men in the world!'

'Ah, well,' said the householder. 'That explains it; I'm hardly in the class of such scholars. He must be way above the likes of ordinary mortals like me!'

Unbeknown to both men, Pandit Vidya Ratan, who was just passing by, stood behind them, listening to their conversation.

'Actually, Sir,' the stranger interposed, 'I am looking for Sri Krishna Dasi. He told me he lived next door to Pandit Vidya Ratan, and that's why I'm trying to find Panditji's house.'

'Sri Krishna Dasi! Why, didn't you say so earlier?' exclaimed the man. 'Why, everyone knows Krishna Dasi. He is everybody's friend, everybody's helper! Come, come, I'll take you to his house right away. I was bewildered when you mentioned some Pandit's name.'

'Sri Krishna Dasi told me to ask for Panditji's house,' the stranger exclaimed. 'He was sure that everyone would know that great, learned man but not many would know him. It appears that he underestimated himself!'

Pandit was amazed at what he heard and realised that selfless service was greater than learning from books and gaining knowledge.

Swami Vivekananda was a great soul who realised this truth perfectly. So he coined the term *Daridra Narayan*, for he beheld God in the poor and the downtrodden.

Once, a group of labourers was summoned to cut and clear away the thick, wild growth of grass and thorny weeds that had grown around Belur Math. When it was time for their midday break, Swamiji himself served them a delicious meal. He sat with them and talked to each one, asking them about their families, their village, their difficulties and problems. He made them feel loved and wanted; he felt himself to be one of them.

'Look at them, how good and innocent they are,' he said to his disciples. 'I wish you would learn to serve them and lessen their miseries. That is real *sanyas*—not just donning your yellow robe. Serve God by serving them!'

Pandit Omkarnath Thakur was visiting the holy city of Haridwar, one of the greatest pilgrimage centres for Hindus in India. As he walked down the banks of the holy Ganga river, the great classical music exponent saw a blind musician, desperately trying to play his *dilruba*.

The Pandit noted that the man's palm was badly injured which was why he was unable to play the instrument.

'Can I help you, my friend?' he asked gently.

'I am in such a fix,' said the blind man. 'The pilgrims pay me some money if I play my instrument. Now, I have hurt myself and I cannot play. It looks as if I will have to starve today!'

'May I try to play your *dilruba,* my friend?' enquired the Pandit. 'It seems to me you have a fine instrument!'

'It is, Brother,' said the blind man with great enthusiasm. 'My father made it for me specially! But do you know how to play it?'

'I can try,' said the great musician. He began to play so beautifully, that before long, a huge appreciative crowd had gathered before them. People showered coins and notes onto the white cloth spread before the blind man.

When the old man had gathered all the money happily, Panditji slipped away quietly.

A Jewish writer tells us the fascinating story of the two seas in Israel. They are both very different.

One is called the Sea of Galilee. It is a large lake with clean fresh water which you can drink. Fish live in it. People swim in it. It is surrounded by green fields and gardens. Many people have built their homes near it. Jesus is said to have sailed across it several times during his earthly sojourn.

The other big body of water is called the Dead Sea. It really lives up to its name. Everything about it is dead. The water is so salty that you would get sick if you try to drink it. It has no fish. Nothing grows along its banks. The water is so 'heavy' that even people who cannot swim actually float in it!

A few tourists who visit the Dead Sea do try to test this—and they float in the Dead Sea. But when they come out, they smell so bad that others stay away from them!

The most interesting thing about the two seas is that the same river flows into both of them—the Jordan river.

The only difference is this: The river flows into the top of the Sea of Galilee and flows out at the bottom.

The river then flows into the Dead Sea and never flows out again.

One receives and gives; the other receives and keeps.

The Dead Sea selfishly keeps the water only for itself. This makes it dead. It gets and never gives!

If you wish to be happy, make others happy!

PART III

Staying Rooted In Calmness

1

You Can Conquer Irritation and Unhappiness!

I have repeatedly said that we live in an age of stress and tension. But I must add here, that what compounds the problem today is the way we react to stressful situations.

Down the ages, and in the deep distant past, annoying, perplexing, frustrating situations have always confronted the best of men. It is not as if we of the modern age have the sole monopoly over stress and tension!

So much so, even the Bhagavad Gita, that Universal Scripture, the Bible of Humanity, tells us about the ideal man—the *stitha prajna*—the man who is calm in wisdom, the man of utter peace of spirit, who lives and moves in peace and has his being rooted in God.

'What are the marks of such a man who is steadfast, concentrated and of illumined consciousness?' Arjuna asks of the Lord.

In his wonderful commentary on the Gita, Sadhu Vaswani tells us that the *stitha prajna* is a man of wisdom—one whose centre is the atman, whose circumference is the wide world.

So let us take note—we are not talking about renunciates who have given up on worldly life when we are talking about the *stitha prajna*; he lives in the world, he deals with his fellow men, but he is *atmavaan*, spirit-centred.

He is a man of detachment. He has renounced desires; he is without *raag* (attraction) and *dvesha* (hatred). He is, thus, free from the dominion of the passions. He is a stranger to fear and anger.

How different is such a man from the unstable individual, who is feeble-minded, prone to violent likes and dislikes! The latter is easily perturbed, constantly in a state of fear, worry, excitement or anger. He is prone to irritation and vexation; he is perpetually restless.

Let us see how Lord Krishna describes the *stitha prajna*, the man of wisdom who is unruffled at all times and in all situations:

- He casts away desires which perturb the mind. He is *nirmohi.*
- He is a man of equanimity. He is free from anxiety amid pains; he is indifferent amid pleasures.
- His understanding is established in wisdom. He has conquered likes and dislikes.
- He is not a man of repression but a man of will power, pure and strong.
- He has an established mind, firmly set in wisdom.

Does this not lead you to ask yourself, 'Why can't more of us be like this ideal man? What is it that makes so many of us restless and unhappy?'

The causes of human restlessness are not far to seek:

- Constant seeking after objects flares up into passion—*kama.*
- When passion is thwarted, there flames up anger—*krodha.*

- Anger leads to loss of reason and sanity, and we pass into a state of delusion—*sanmoha.*
- In this state of delusion, we lose our memory—*smriti.* We lose the memory of our Guru's *upadesh*—the memory of our life's great ideals.
- Losing this memory, we also lose the power of discrimination; we lose reason—*buddhi.*

Let me sum up, in the words of Sadhu Vaswani:

> When the mind is bewildered, confused, you forget the lesson of experience, that is loss of memory. Forgetting experience, you lose discrimination. Losing discrimination, you miss the purpose of life. It is the real loss of man himself.

So the question is—how can we stop ourselves from losing our very humanity? Lives of great men all remind us we can make our lives sublime.

Think of Sri Rama. He is preparing for his coronation as *Yuvaraj* of Ayodhya. Early in the morning on the appointed day, when he has bathed in sanctified waters and dressed in his new, silken royal robes, he is summoned to go to his father, King Dasharatha. As he rides in his princely chariot, he sees the city radiant with joy and celebration; the people cheer him on his way, assuming that the holy rituals of the coronation are about to begin.

Alas, reality is different. You know the familiar story—Sri Rama is told by Kaikeyi that he must give up his right to the throne and go into the forest as an exile, for fourteen long years.

Just think of this. What would your reaction be if your brother takes away your bike and you are forced to take a bus to college?

How would you feel if your mother told you to take your grandfather to the doctor, instead of going out with your friends?

What would you say if your professor announces that he is holding a special class on Sunday?

What do you feel when the electricity fails as you are watching the final moments of a one-day cricket match?

You know the answers as well as I do! We all rave and rant and curse and scowl and otherwise exhibit disagreeable behaviour in such situations.

But Sri Rama—the *Maryada Purushottam* or ideal man that he was, did not so much as flinch! We are told that when he left Kaikeyi's palace, he did not ride in his chariot, for mentally, he had already renounced his royal life!

Did he not have provocation enough to rage and protest? Why, when Lakshmana heard the news, his anger was uncontrollable? When Bharata returned from his trip, he was so incensed by his mother's deed that he cursed her and turned his back upon her for making him the pretext of her terrible scheme!

But Sri Rama remained unperturbed, calm, unmoved—exemplifying the *stitha prajna.* What a glorious example for us to cherish!

Consider Jesus Christ. He knew all that was to come—that before the cock crowed thrice, he would be denied by his own arch disciple; that he would be sold for thirty pieces of silver by one whom he trusted and loved. Yet what did he do? He washed the feet of his disciples with his own hands and symbolically offered them his life, his flesh and blood in the unforgettable Last Supper.

Consider Prophet Muhammad. In his early days as the Messenger of Allah, he faced the enmity and hostility of powerful men who were out to kill him. They spread vicious rumours against him, they called him an atheist, they heaped insult and slander on the Prophet. Even the children on the road, we are told, took up stones to throw at him!

Unmoved, unflinching, the Prophet stood by the truth he believed in.

Think of Gautama the Buddha, in the days when countless men flocked to him and began to follow him. The rich, the powerful and the nobly born, all renounced their lives of comfort and ease to embrace his order and become bhikkus, cheerfully accepting the rigours of a homeless life.

Gautama's cousin Devadatta was jealous of the Buddha's growing eminence. Infatuated with the lust for power, he even schemed to put an end to his cousin's life. He set a fierce and wild elephant loose on the Buddha's path.

As people panicked and fled in all directions, the Buddha stood still and calm. There was a heavenly loveliness in his face, a divine light in his eyes. With infinite compassion, he said to his terrified disciples, 'Fear not, my brethren! He who harms none, will be harmed by no one!'

The magic of the Master's presence not only tamed the raging elephant and made it docile; it also transformed the soul of his wicked cousin Devadatta, who sought his forgiveness and became his devout disciple.

Think of Socrates, whose sole mission in life was to urge his fellow Athenians on the path of right thinking and right conduct. He had some of the greatest and wisest men of his age as his followers, yet, he founded no school of philosophy. He merely questioned and reasoned and tried to lead men towards the light. But the powerful nobles of the day brought him to trial, accusing him of disbelieving the Gods and corrupting the youth.

After a grossly unfair trial, he was condemned to die by drinking hemlock—the Athenian method of capital punishment. The great philosopher accepted the verdict calmly. In a dignified farewell message, he bid adieu to the court which had sentenced him to death. 'Now, it is time to depart, for me to die, for you to live,' he concluded, 'But which of us is going to a better state is unknown to everyone but God.'

The death of Socrates is movingly narrated by his disciple Plato. He drank the poison calmly, urged his friends not to regret his loss and asked them to withhold their grief so that he could die in peace and quiet.

It is said that a physiognomist who once saw Socrates took a good look at his rolling eyes, thick lips, flat nose and short, thickset figure and said, 'This man is of a licentious disposition; he must be one of the most depraved, corrupt and immodest men in the world.'

The great philosopher's admirers nearly murdered the man. But Socrates held them in check, and remarked, 'All that the man said is true but I have curbed and corrected my vicious propensities by means of reason.'

There are many ignoble tendencies, many negative emotions which dwell in all of us. We must rule them and check them not only by the strength of reason and will power but also by the exercise of the spirit, by greatness of soul.

It is a sad fact of life that the greatest souls born among us cannot always escape the slander, malice and calumny of the envious. My beloved Master, Sadhu Vaswani, was no exception.

Thus, it was that an editor of a newspaper in Hyderabad-Sind began to heap slander and abuse on Sadhu Vaswani. Envious of the Master's good name and his saintly reputation, the editor published several false news reports against him and his satsang. He even had the newspaper distributed for free in several houses to spread his slanderous attacks.

Deeply disturbed by this unprovoked malice, some of the devotees spoke about it to Sadhu Vaswani but he only smiled and did not take it to heart. Nor would he let them utter even a word against the man who had slandered him so viciously.

A few days passed and the editor was beset with personal problems. He faced great difficulties and hardships and simply did not know where to turn for help.

When Sadhu Vaswani came to know of this, he visited the man in his home and spoke to him in love and kindness. He also did his best to redress the man's difficulties. The man was so overwhelmed that he fell at Sadhu Vaswani's feet and began to weep tears of bitter repentance. The Master picked him up and embraced him lovingly.

How kind, compassionate, ever-loving are the wise and holy ones! They teach us to foster love and grace and good feelings in place of our negativism and dark emotions.

'Love, love, love thine enemies,' Sadhu Vaswani said, 'and though they hate thee as a thorn, thou wilt bloom as a rose.'

That is the secret of a happy, carefree, stress-free life: Love life; love your fellow human beings; love this beautiful world you live in; above all, love the Lord, and you too will bloom like a rose!